I0461816

Guitar Folksong Duets
For Pupil and Teacher
Volume 3

By Adrian Allan

Edited by Allan H. Jones

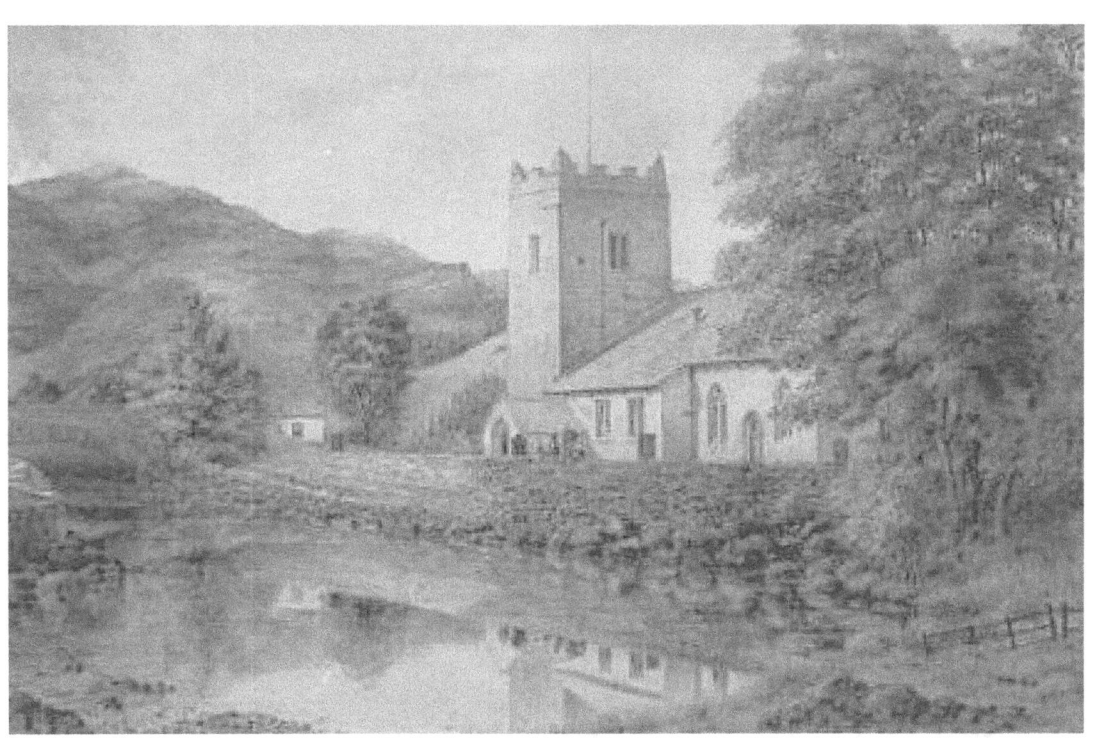

Meadow Music Publishing

First Edition: 2018

ISBN: 978-0-244-99011-4

Meadow Music Publishing
23c Burford Rd
Manchester, M16 8EW

adrianallan12345@gmail.com

www.facebook.com/meadowmusicpublishing/

Front cover: anonymous watercolour, c.1914

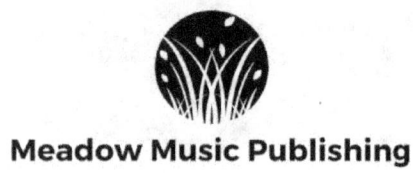

Meadow Music Publishing

Contents

Preface

This third volume of folksong duets for pupil and teacher offers a range of music from around the world. Some pieces contain strong national elements, such as *Sakura* and *If You Want To Write To Me*. As in the previous volumes, the music covers a range of early-stage abilities, from the most simple of melodies, such as *Go To Sleep*, to more challenging syncopations found in *Mwana Wange*. The book is also suitable for intermediate players (grade 3-6); they can attempt the teacher parts, or sight-read the pupil parts.

A note on the music

Blow Away The Morning Dew is an English song that tells of a meeting between a maid and a knight. It was first written down in 1719.

Blow The Wind Southerly. This air is from Tyneside in northern England. It was popularised in the last century by the great contralto from Blackburn, Lancashire - Kathleen Ferrier. The teacher part is quite dense, using a counter-melody. It is important to play this *leggiero*, so as not to detract from the main melody line.

Carol is from the Netherlands, and is about baby Jesus; "Here lies this little one, all in the cold".

Go To Sleep is a haunting lullaby from Sweden.

Grass So Green uses a polka rhythm, a dance form that originated in the Czech Republic. Many songs from here are about the nation's agriculture. In this case, the singer asks who will mow his fields while he is away on military service.

If You Want To Write To Me is from the time of the Spanish Civil War. It has a very definite national flavour, and includes rich strummed chords in the accompaniment.

Kaiyeu Nanu is sung by the Maasai children of Kenya when they leave home for boarding school. It has some unusual features (to Western ears), such as five-bar phrase.

Kum By Ya is a very popular hymn that hails from Nigeria.

Kum Bachur Atzel is an Israeli round about a rooster, "hear the rooster crowing, get up without delay". To convey the idea of a round, the accompaniment is notated at one point in three voices.

Look Mr Cuckoo is a simple children's song from Finland.

Mwana Wange is a song that is sung by the Buganda people in Uganda. It includes some unusual syncopations that some players will find a challenge.

Mother Volga is less well known than the *Song of the Volga Boatmen*, but was also probably sung while pulling barges on the Russian river.

Old Dan Tucker is an American nonsense song from the frontier days. The accompaniment is quite "full", so needs to be played lightly.

Sakura is one of the most famous national songs of Japan. It depicts spring, the season of cherry blossoms. The melody is pentatonic, and the intervals in the accompaniment reflect an oriental tonality.

Suliram is a lullaby from Indonesia that says, "Go to sleep, little baby. Now that you're here, I want to keep you with me".

The Colorado Trail is a popular cowboy song. The trail itself is a long distance route around the Rocky Mountains in Colorado, spanning 486 miles.

The Four Marys tells of the demise of Mary Hamilton, one of the four ladies-in-waiting to Mary, Queen of Scots.

The Maid Of Leko is a German folk song that tells of a legend where a horseman who pursues the fair maid of the island of Leko. Both the maid and the horseman were turned into stone.

The Mountains Of Mourne is a perennial Irish favourite. The same melody is also known as *Bendemeer's Stream*. It describes the longing of an immigrant to London, for the mountains of his homeland in County Down in Northern Ireland. Guitarists might be interested to know that the composer Fernando Sor used the tune for one of his celebrated studies for the guitar.

The Old Soldier describes the lives of the Klephts, the guerillas who lived in the Greek mountains and defended the land against the Turkish invaders.

The Seeds Of Love uses the metaphor of planting seeds to describe the various "false lovers" on offer to the protagonist of the song. It was collected by Cecil Sharp from an English gardener.

The Trees They Do Grow High is a very popular English ballad. It tells the story of an arranged marriage of a girl to a boy who is even younger than she. It has been recorded by Joan Baez and Martin Carthy.

When Johnny Comes Marching Home is from the time of the American Civil War. It was first published in 1863 as sheet music and expressed the desire for friends to return who were caught up in the war.

Whistle, Daughter, Whistle is a Southern Mountain song from America. The mother of the protagonist advises, "Whistle, daughter, whistle, and you shall have a man".

Wondrous Love is an America spiritual. The love is created by "the Lord", who sends, "such perfect peace".

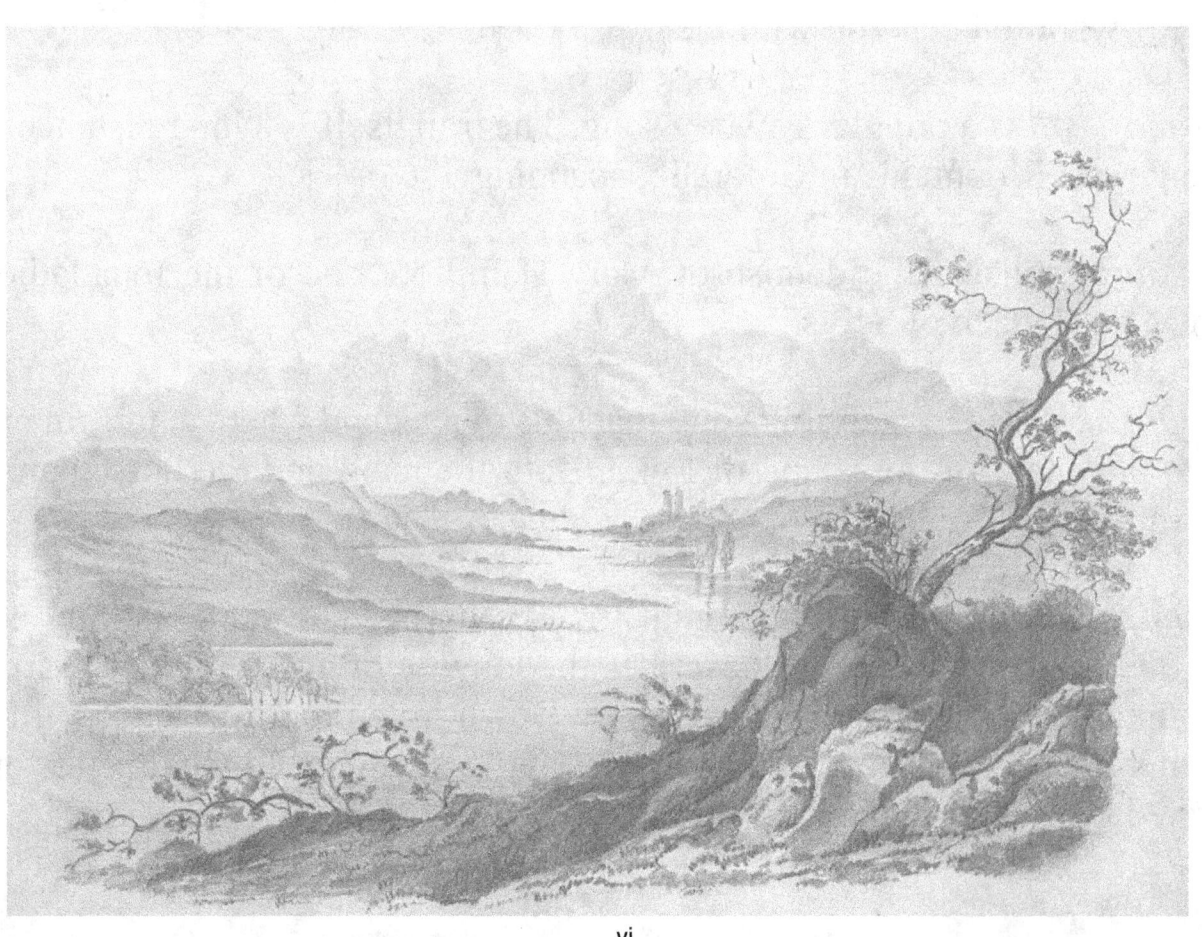

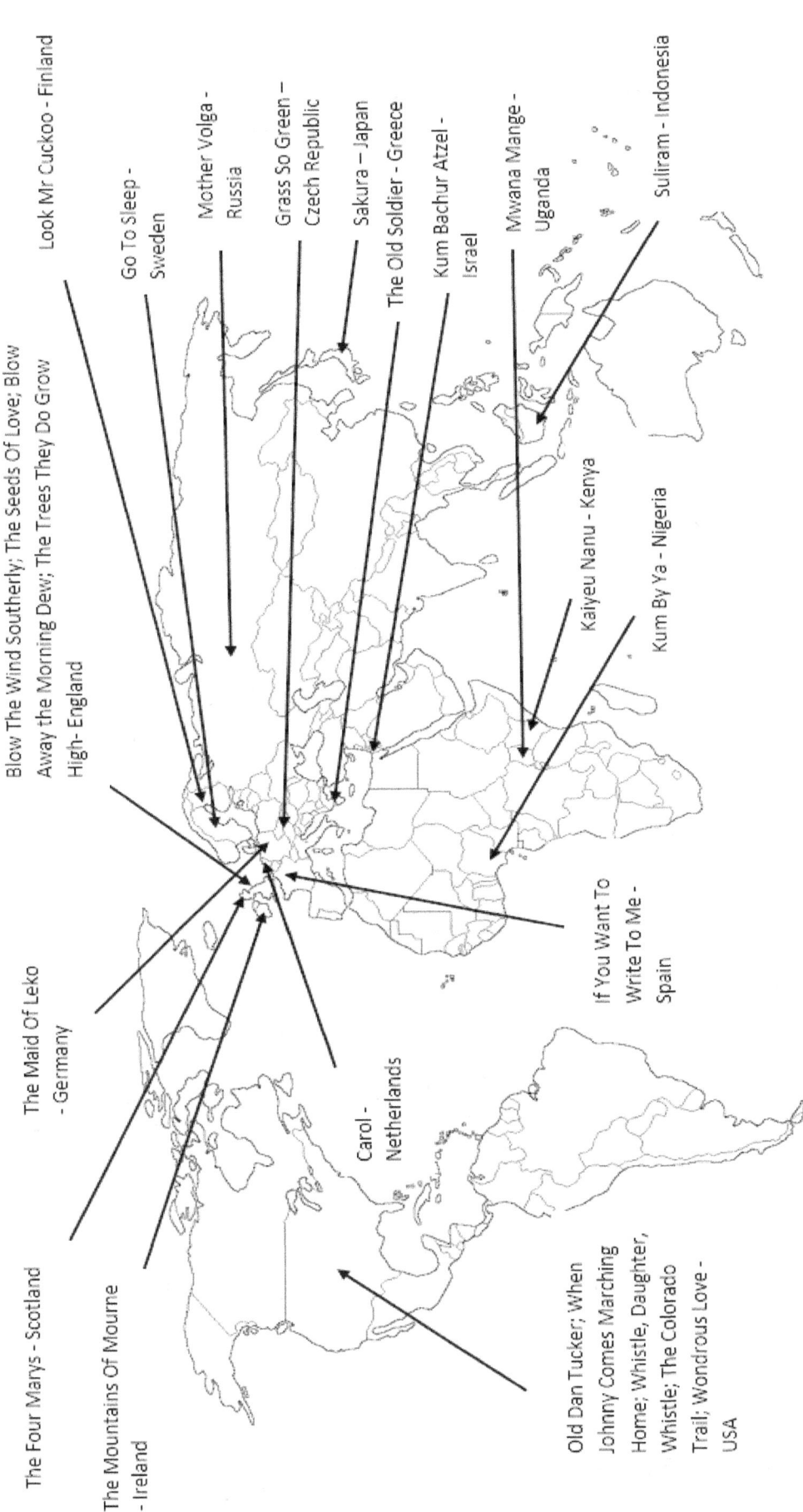

Origin of Songs in This Book

Look Mr Cuckoo - Finland

Go To Sleep - Sweden

Mother Volga - Russia

Grass So Green – Czech Republic

Sakura – Japan

The Old Soldier - Greece

Kum Bachur Atzel - Israel

Mwana Mange - Uganda

Suliram - Indonesia

Blow The Wind Southerly; The Seeds Of Love; Blow Away the Morning Dew; The Trees They Do Grow High- England

Kaiyeu Nanu - Kenya

Kum By Ya - Nigeria

If You Want To Write To Me - Spain

The Maid Of Leko - Germany

The Four Marys - Scotland

The Mountains Of Mourne - Ireland

Carol - Netherlands

Old Dan Tucker; When Johnny Comes Marching Home; Whistle, Daughter, Whistle; The Colorado Trail; Wondrous Love - USA

Blow Away The Morning Dew

Traditional English

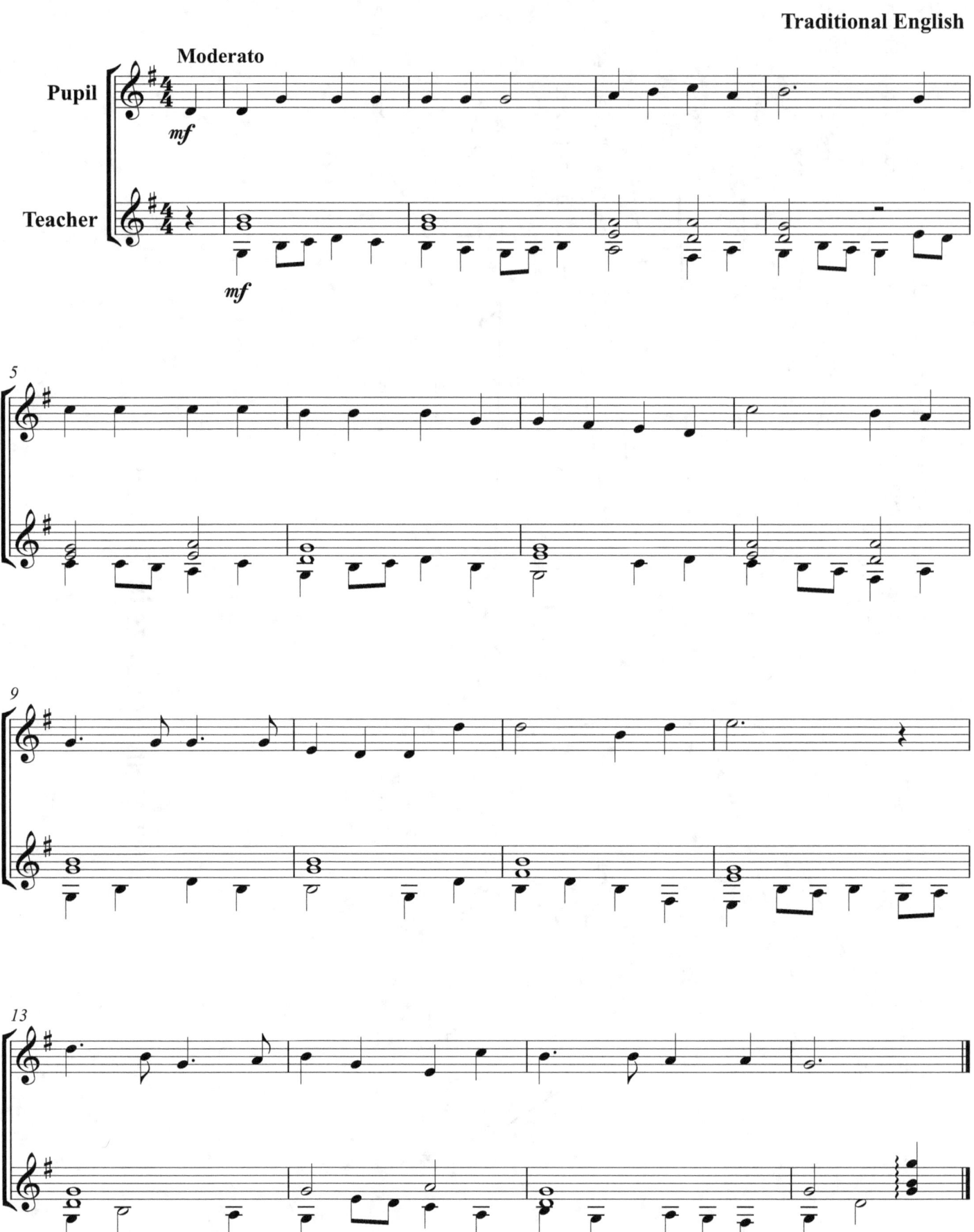

Blow The Wind Southerly

Traditional English

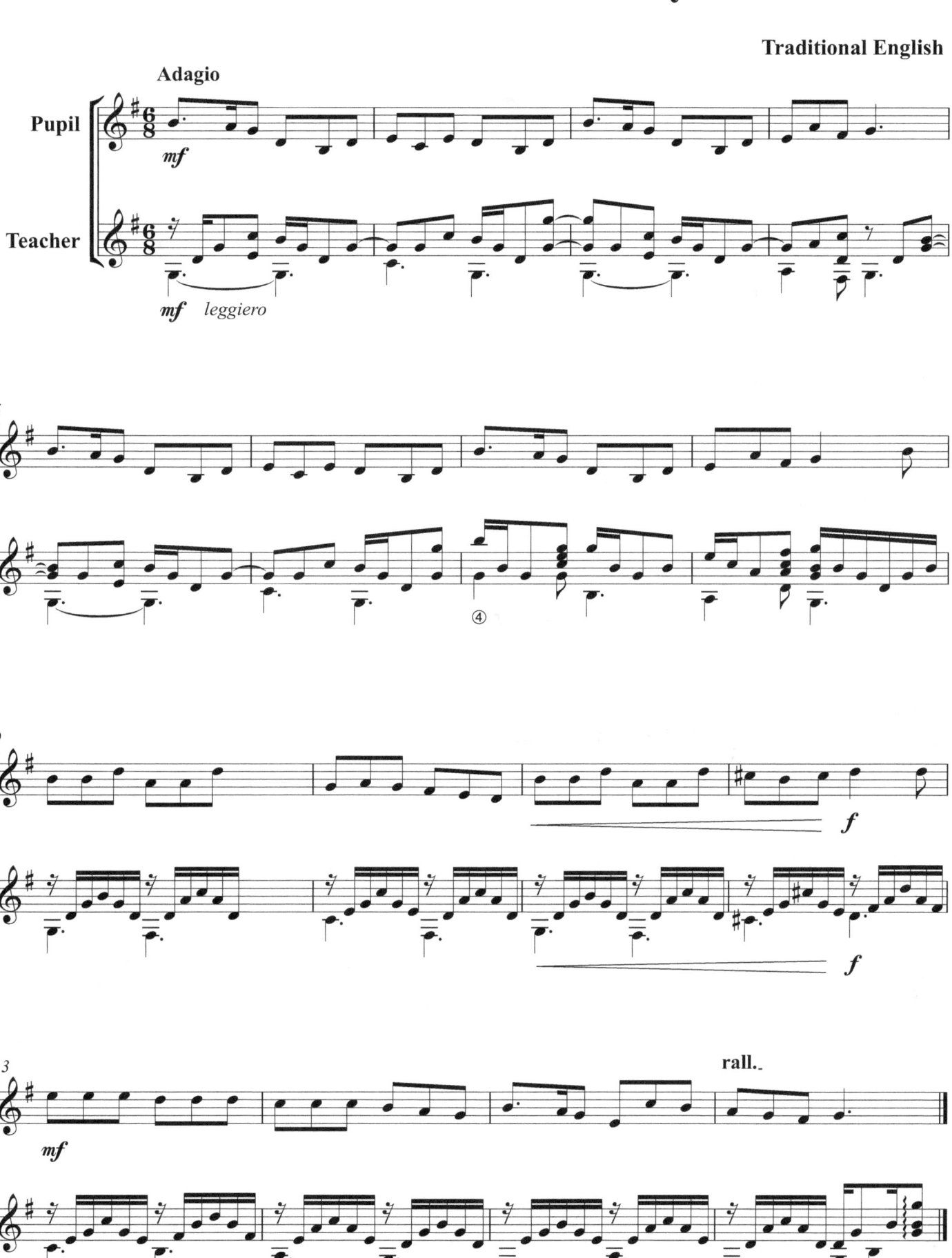

Carol

Traditional Dutch

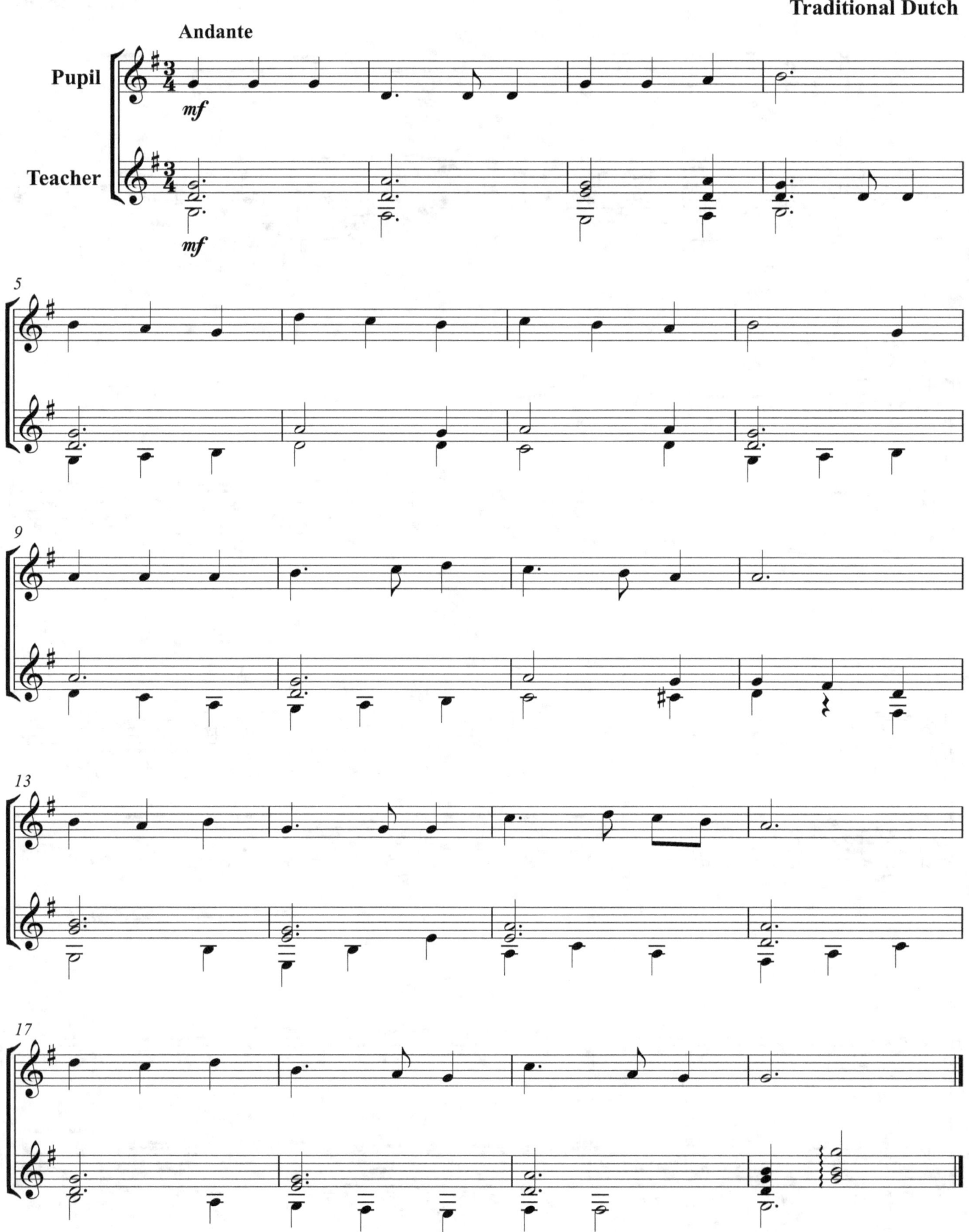

3

Go To Sleep

Traditional Swedish

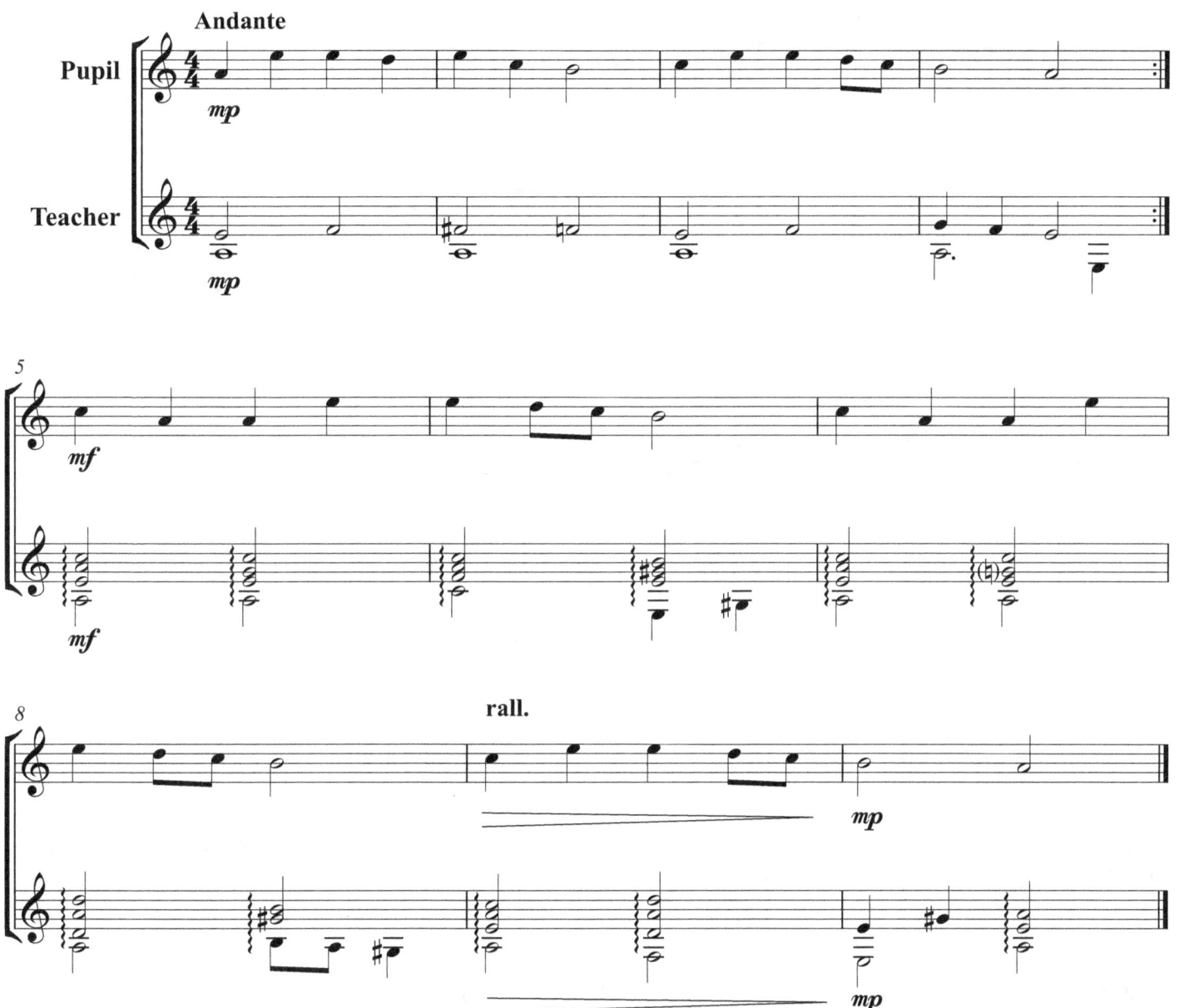

Grass So Green

Traditional Czech

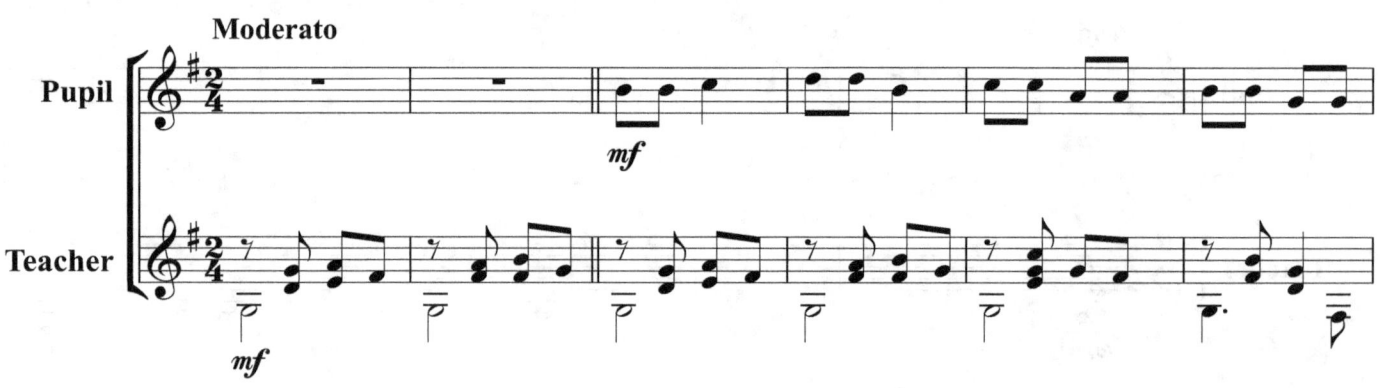

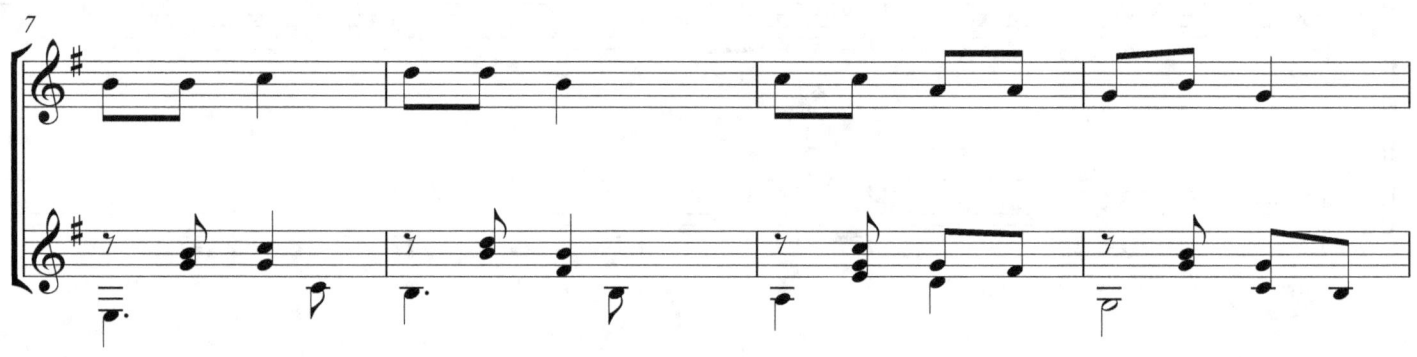

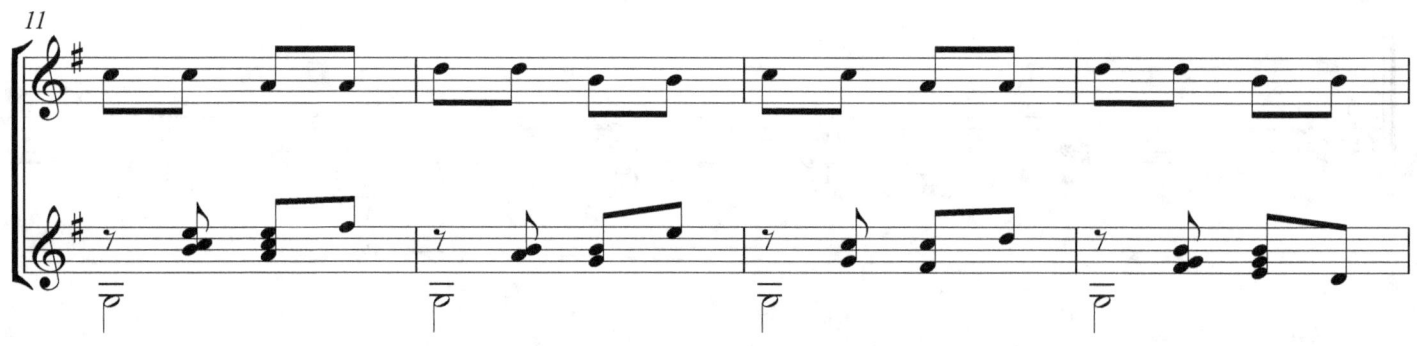

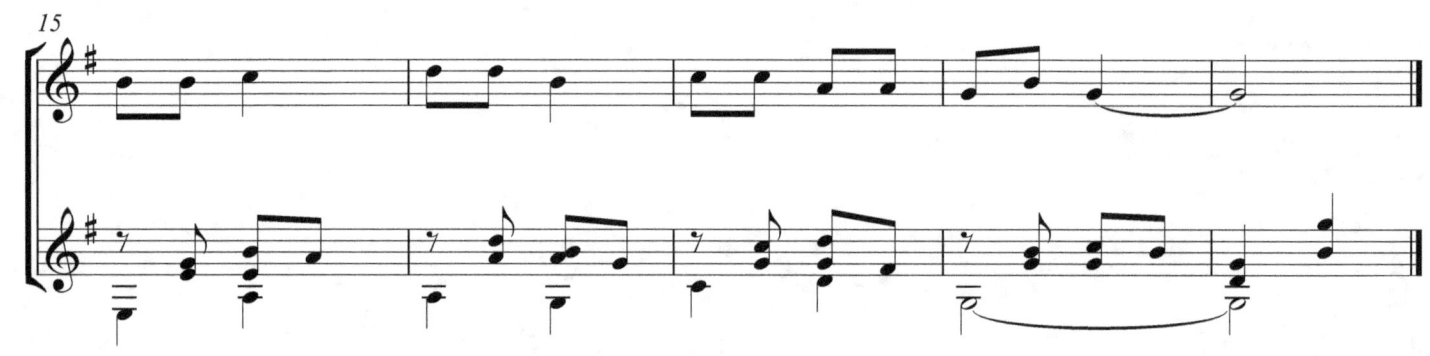

If You Want To Write To Me

Spanish Civil War Song

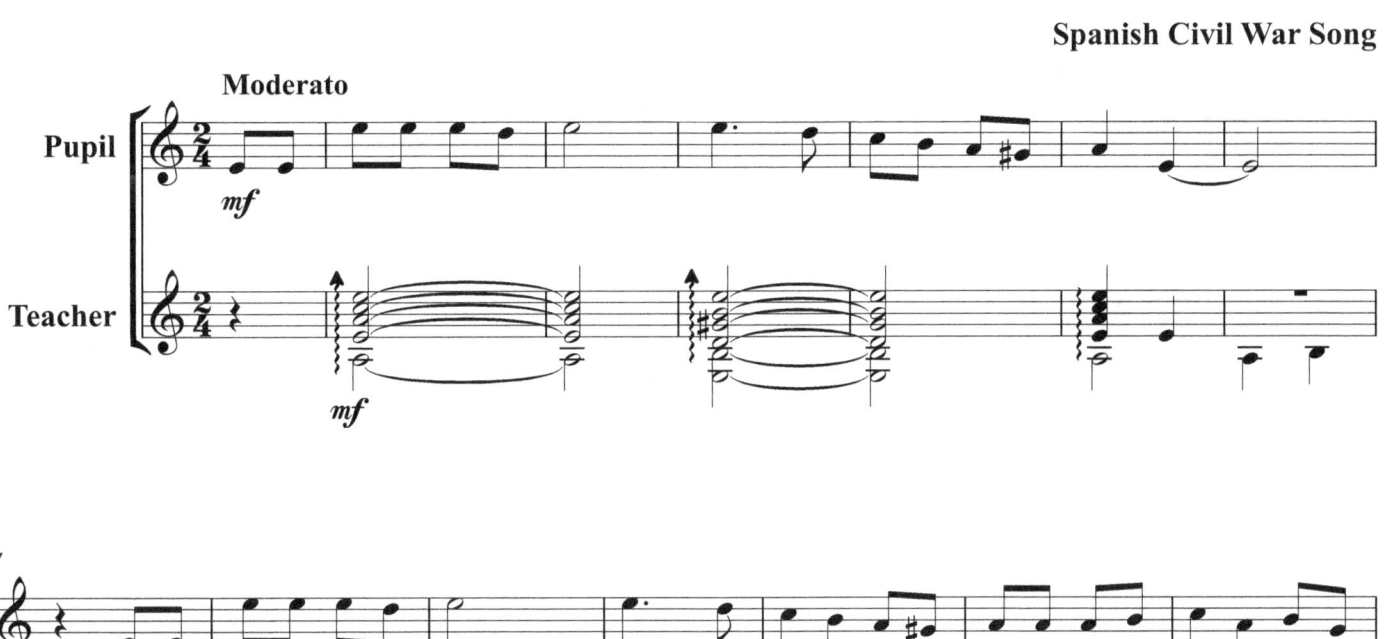

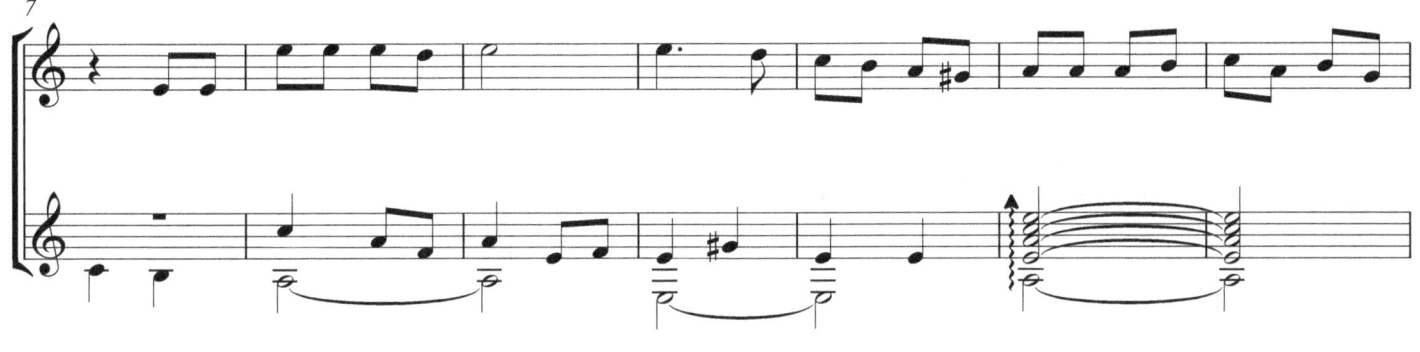

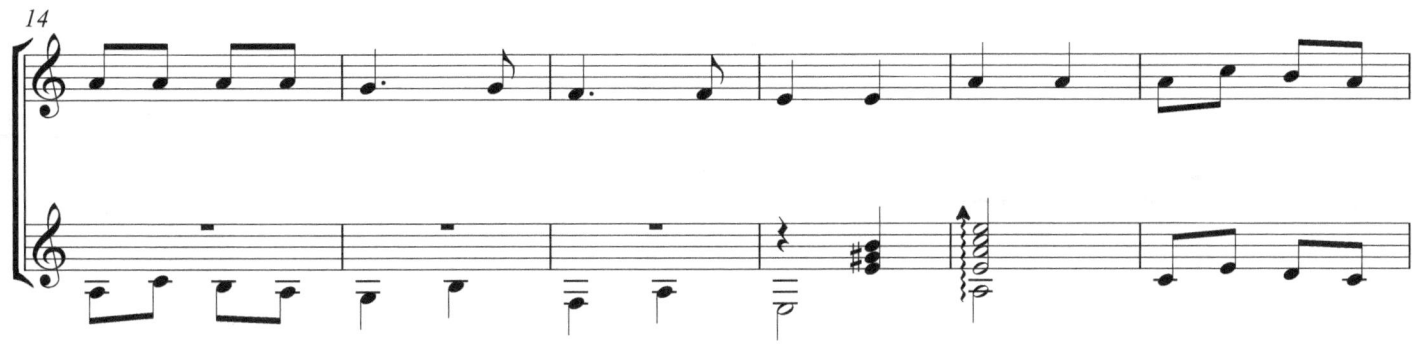

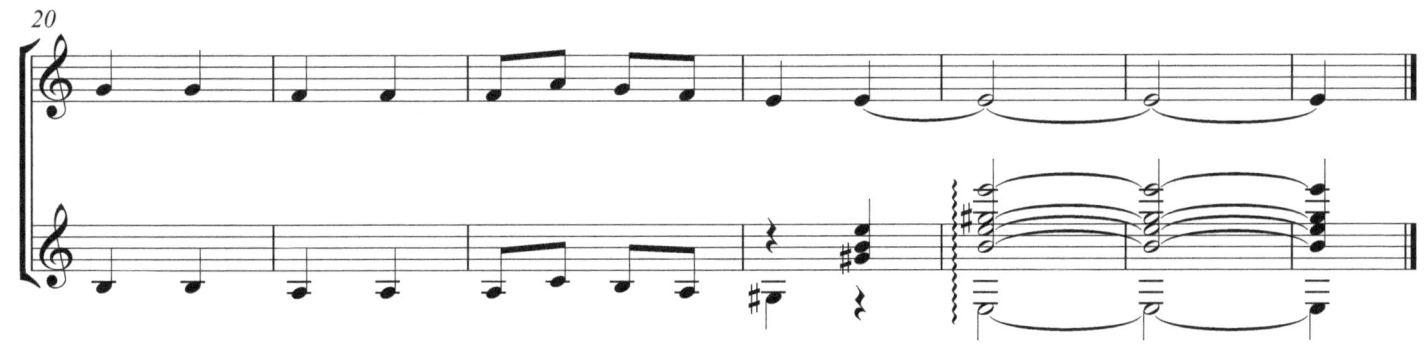

Kaiyeu Nanu

Traditional Kenyan

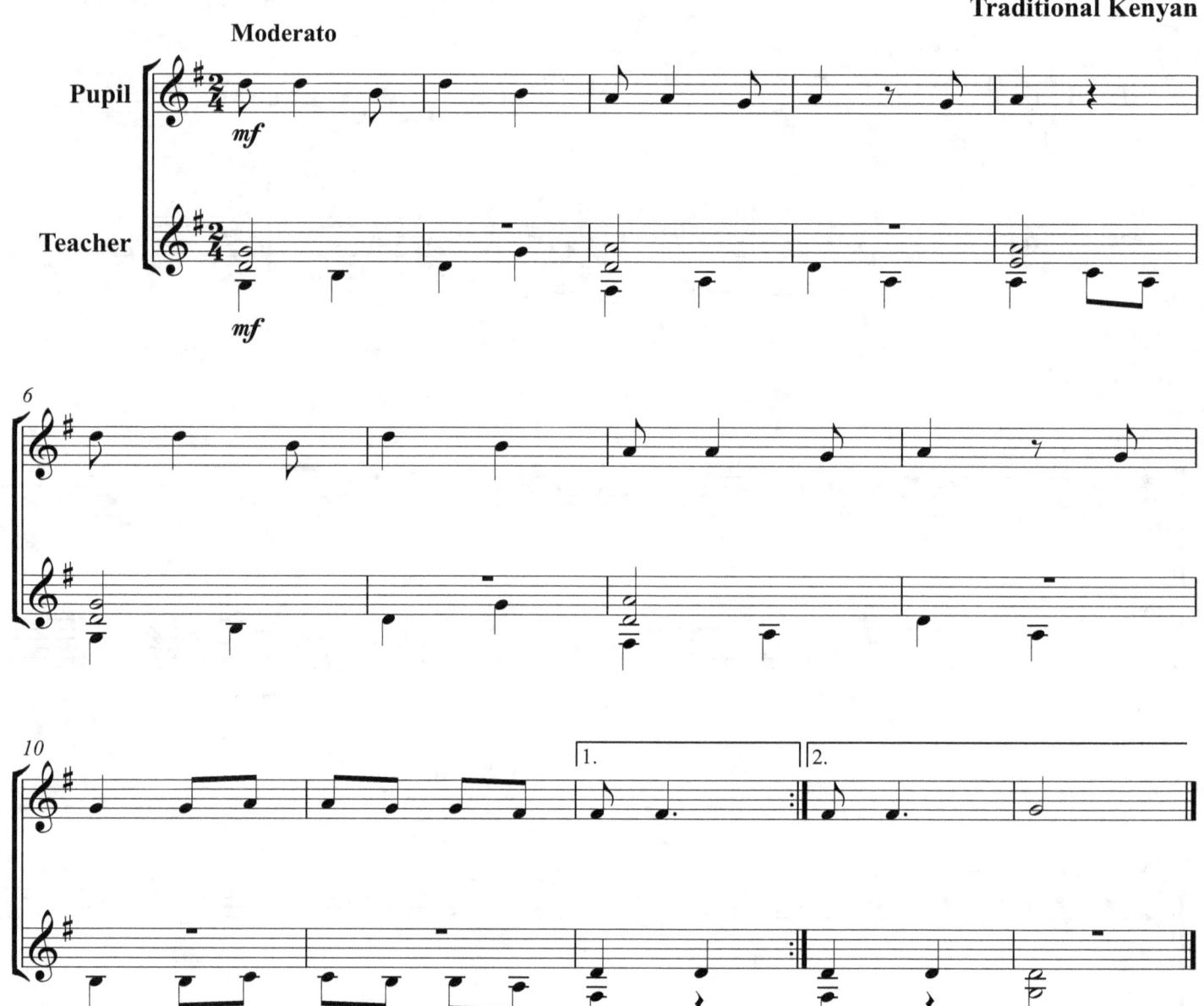

Kum Ba Ya

Traditional Nigerian

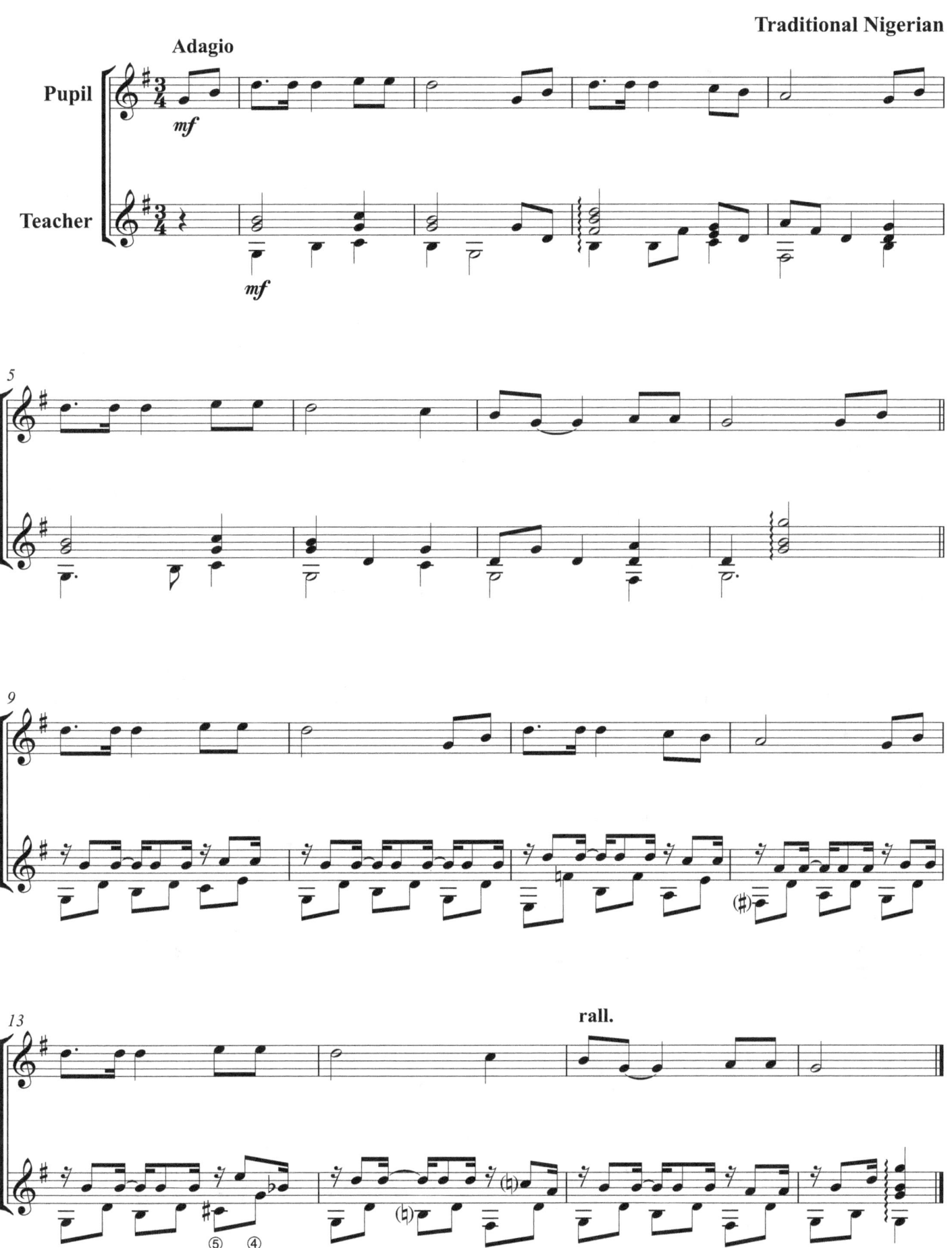

Mwana Wange

Traditional Ugandan

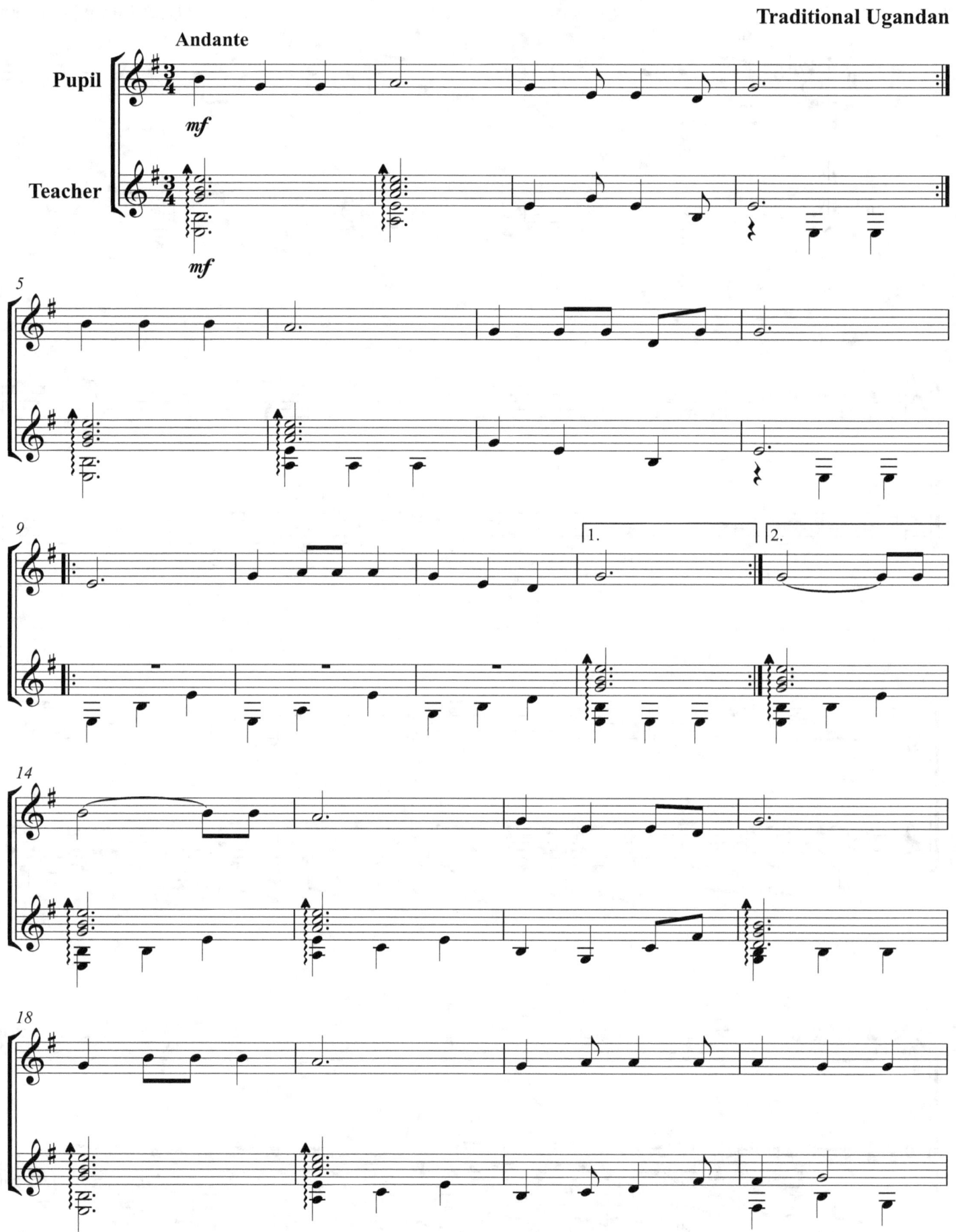

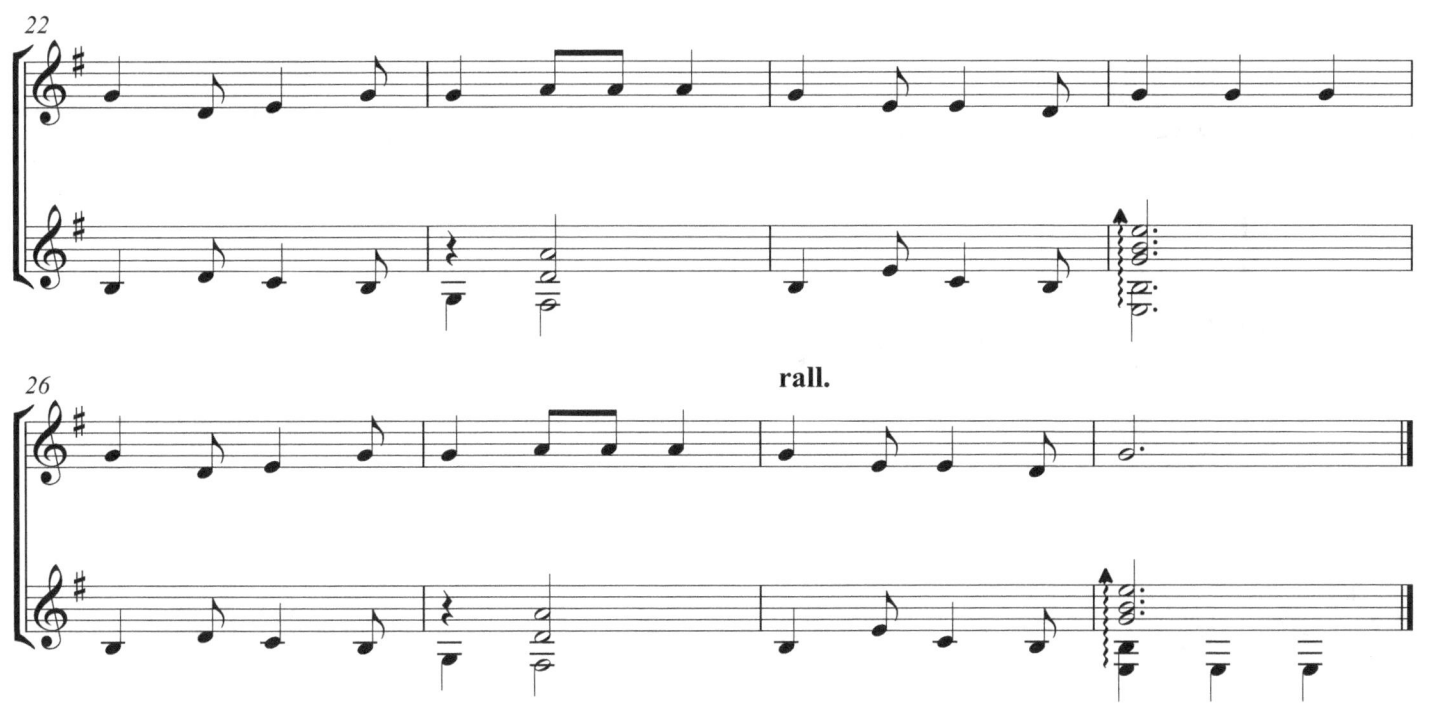

rall.

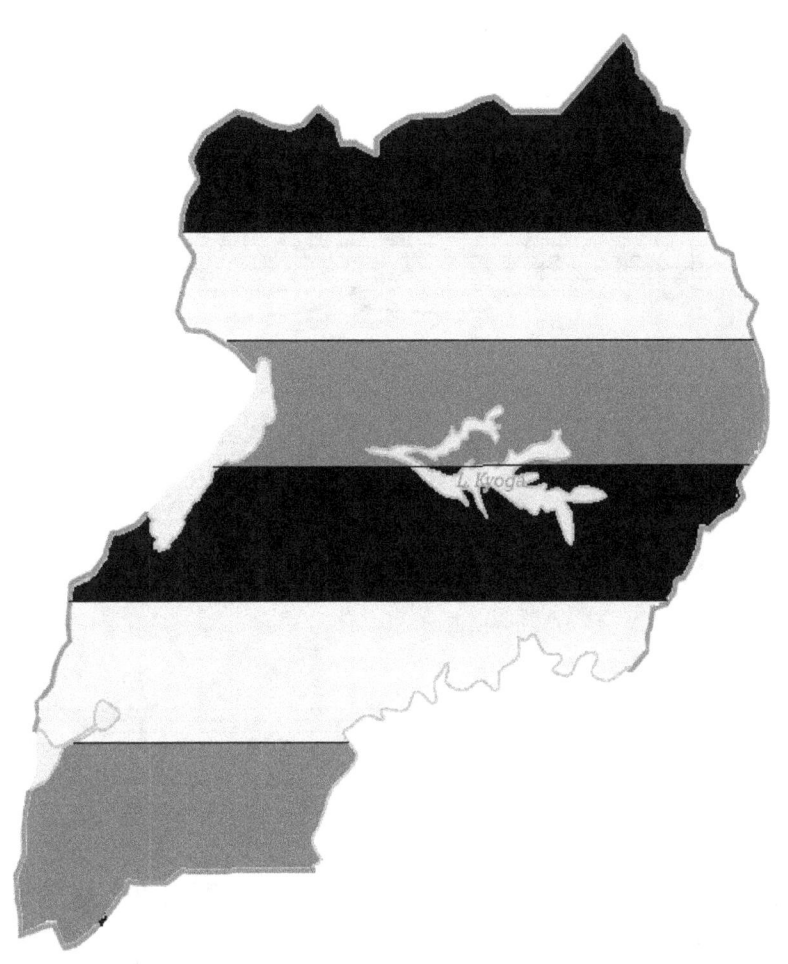

Old Dan Tucker

Traditional American

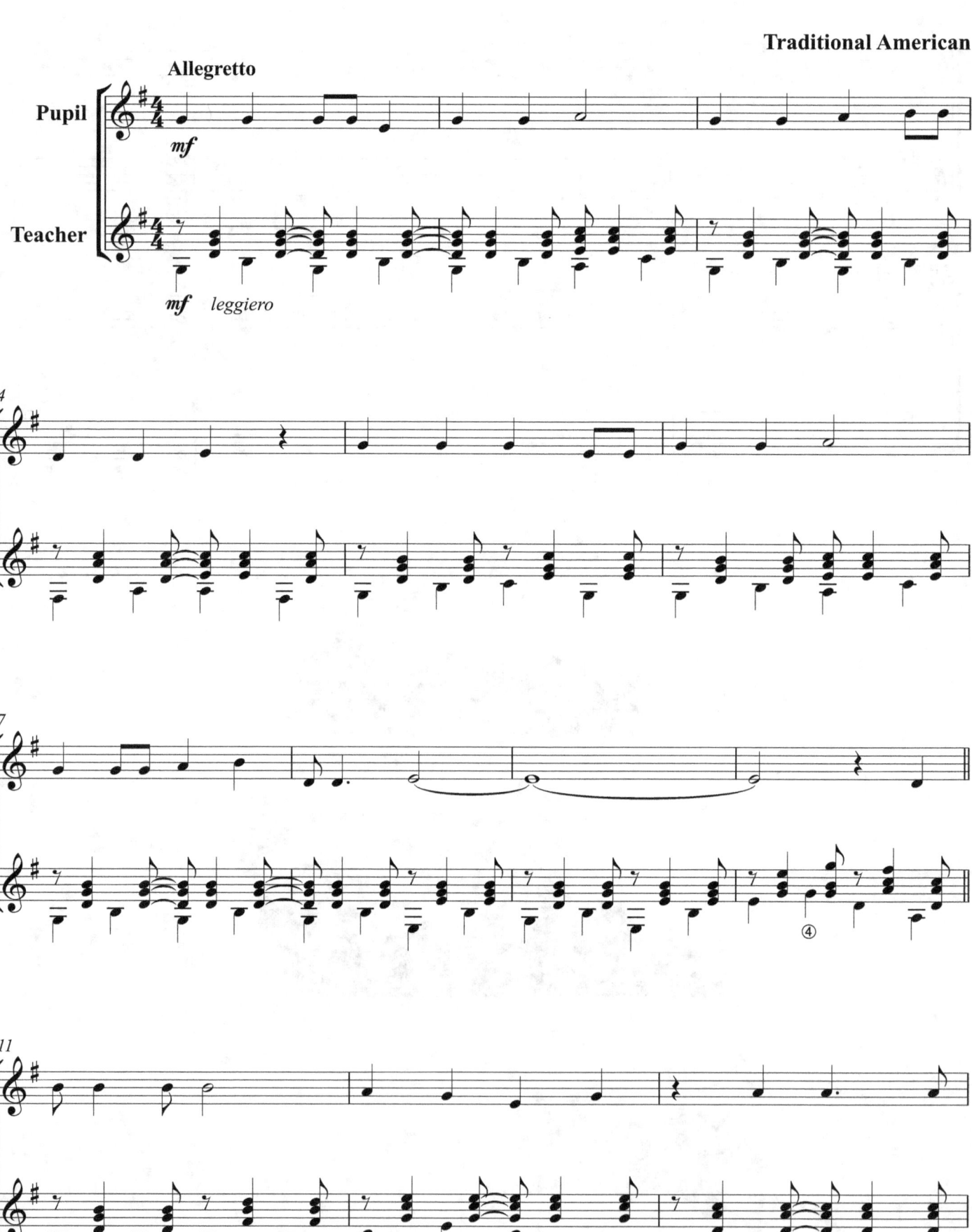

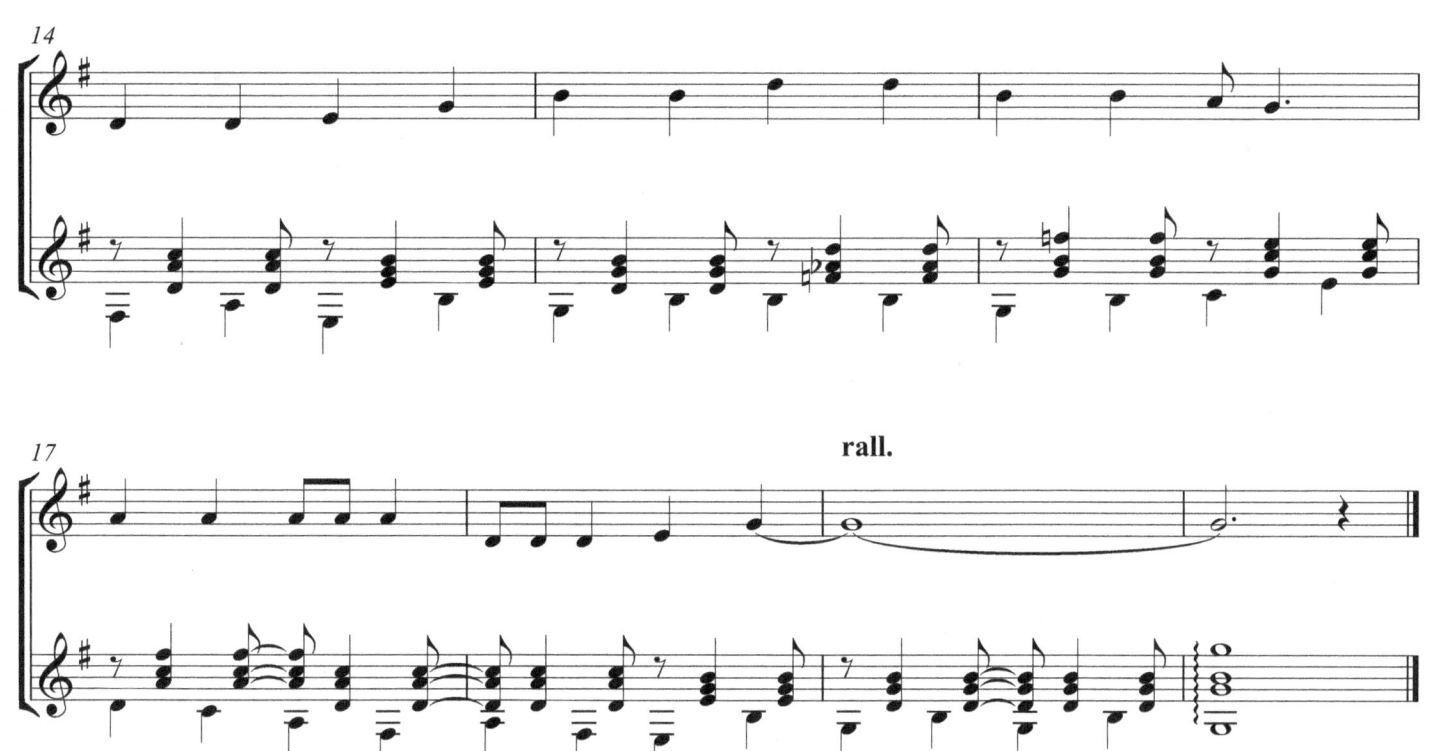

rall.

Kum Bachur Atzel

Traditional Israeli

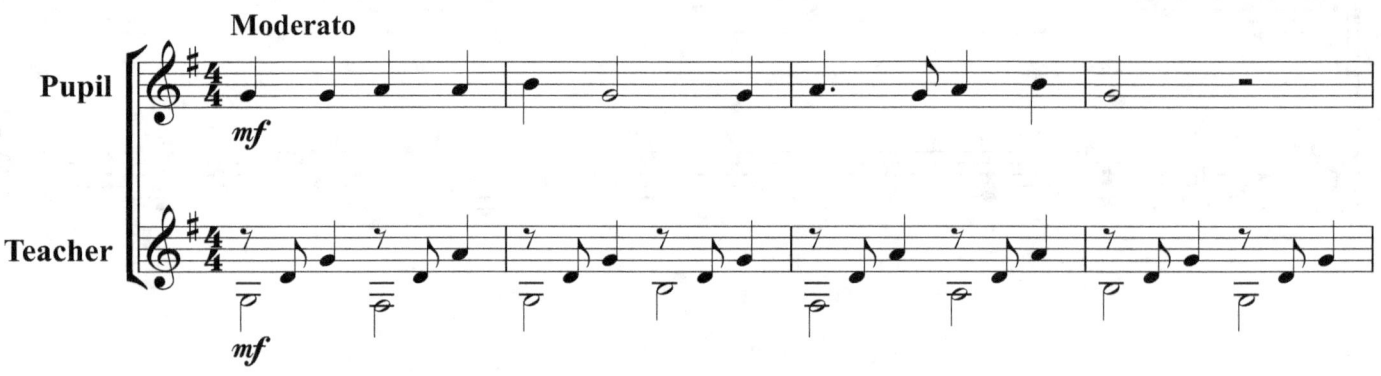

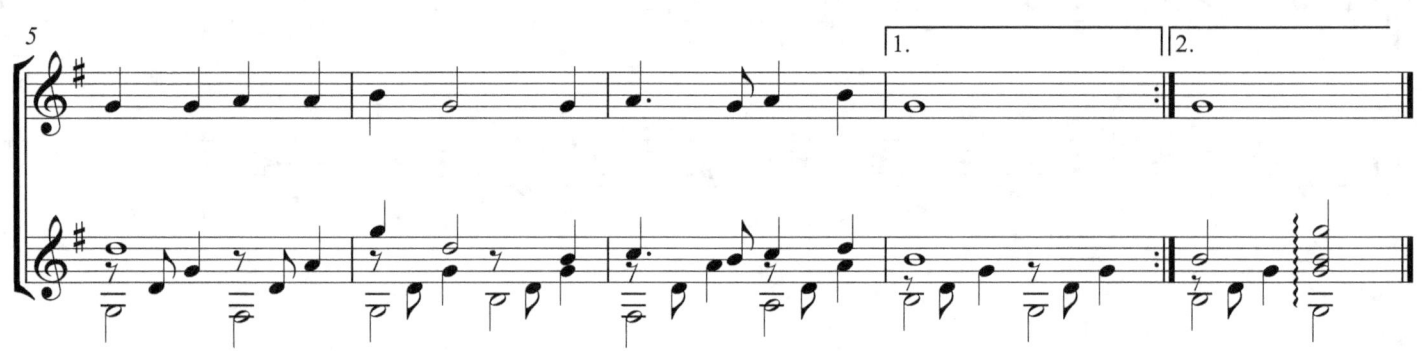

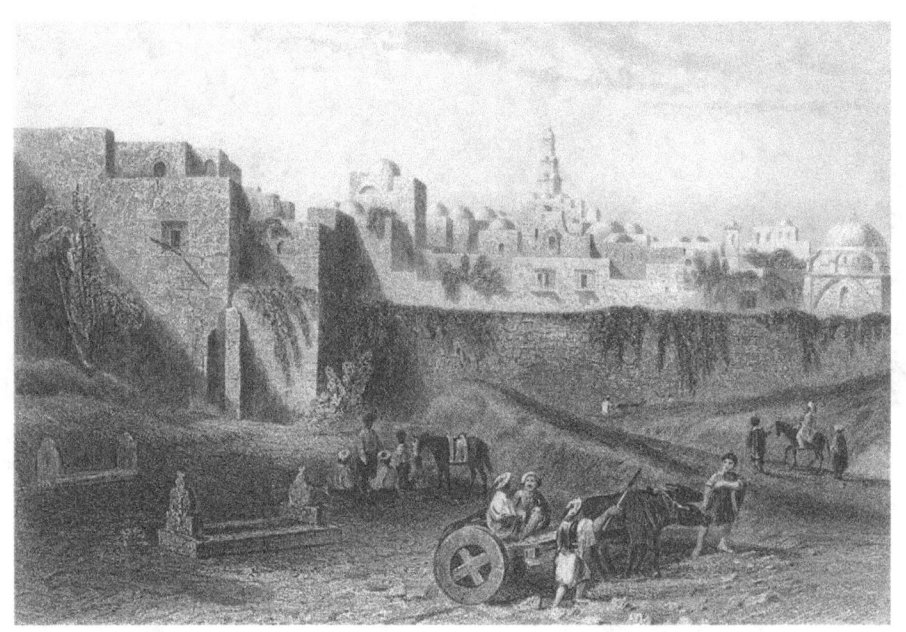

Old Jerusalem

Look Mister Cuckoo

Traditional Finnish

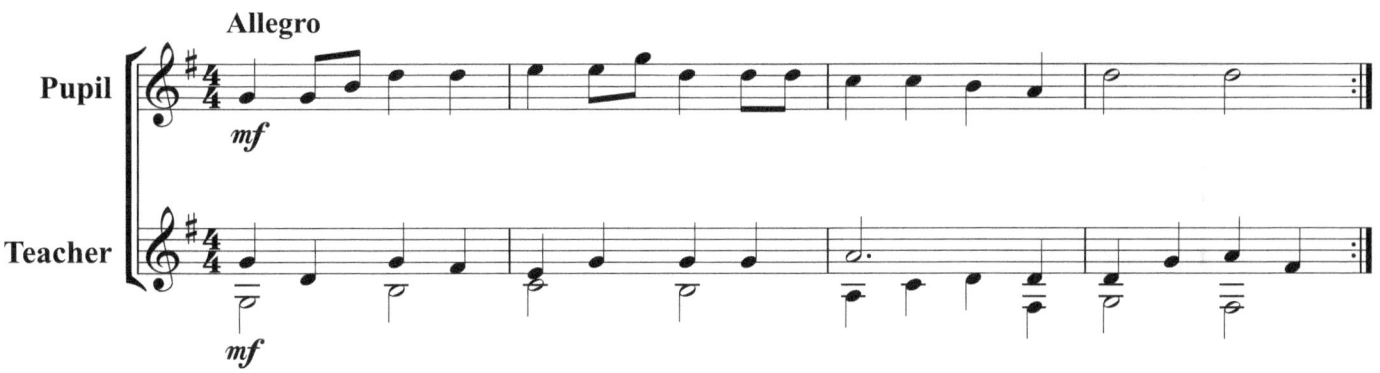

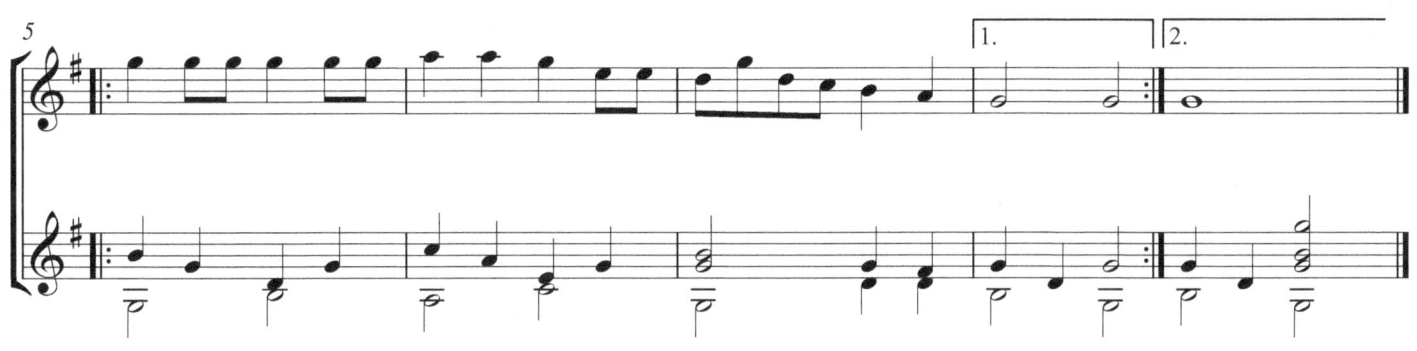

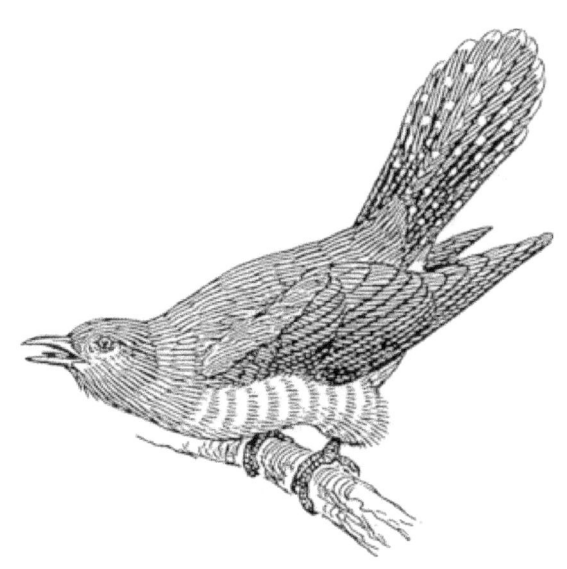

Mother Volga

Traditional Russian

Sakura

Traditional Japanese

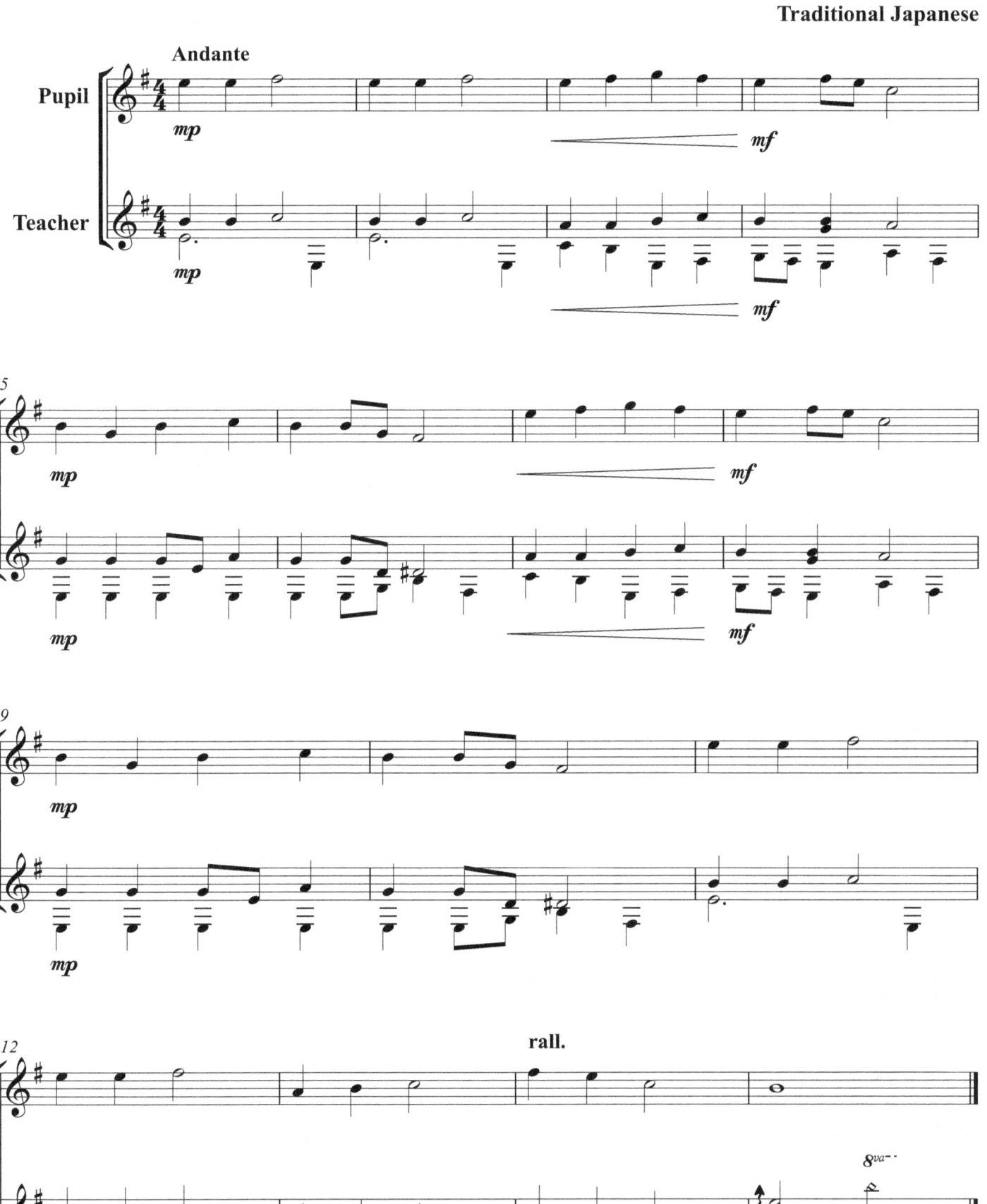

Suliram

Traditional Indonesian

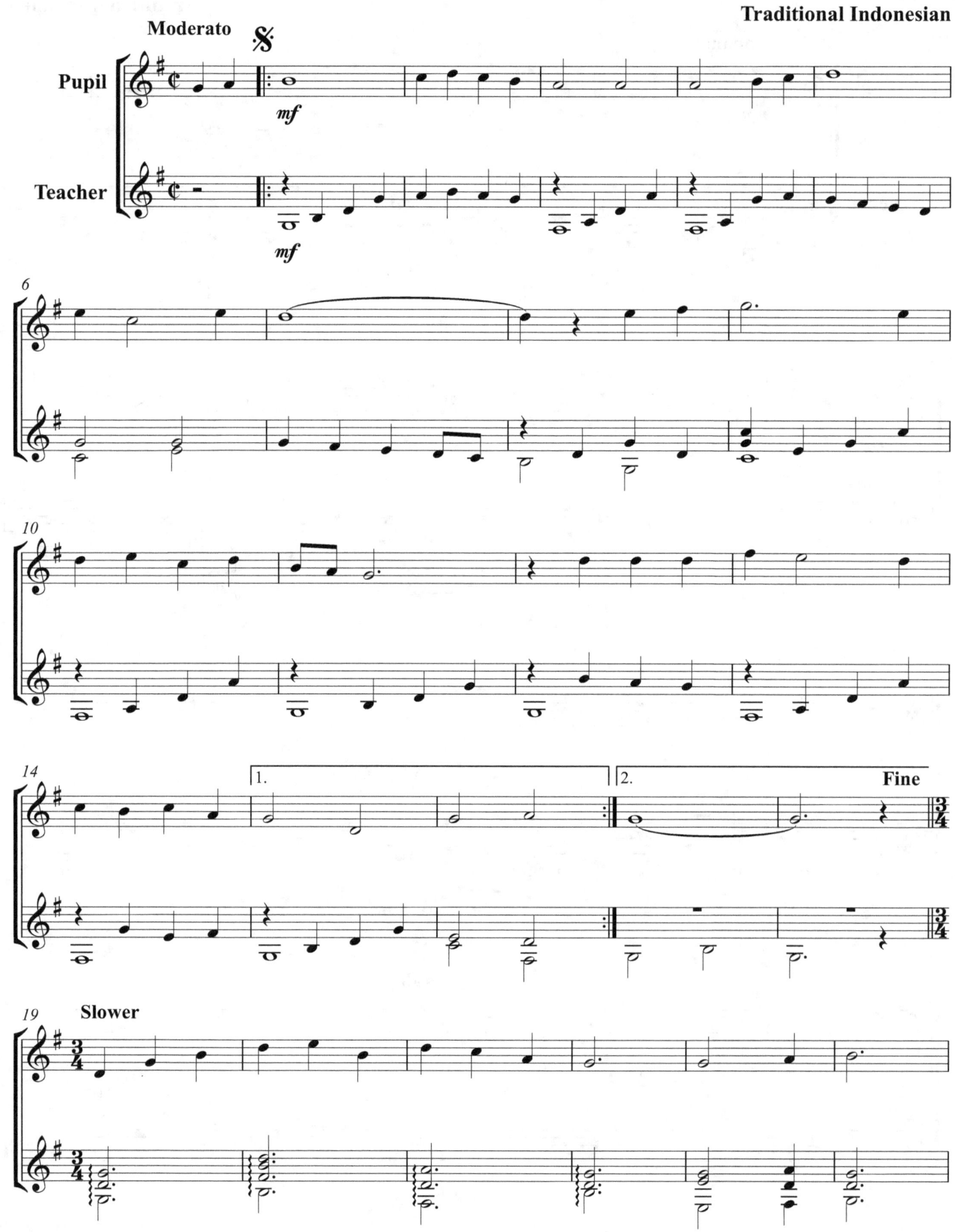

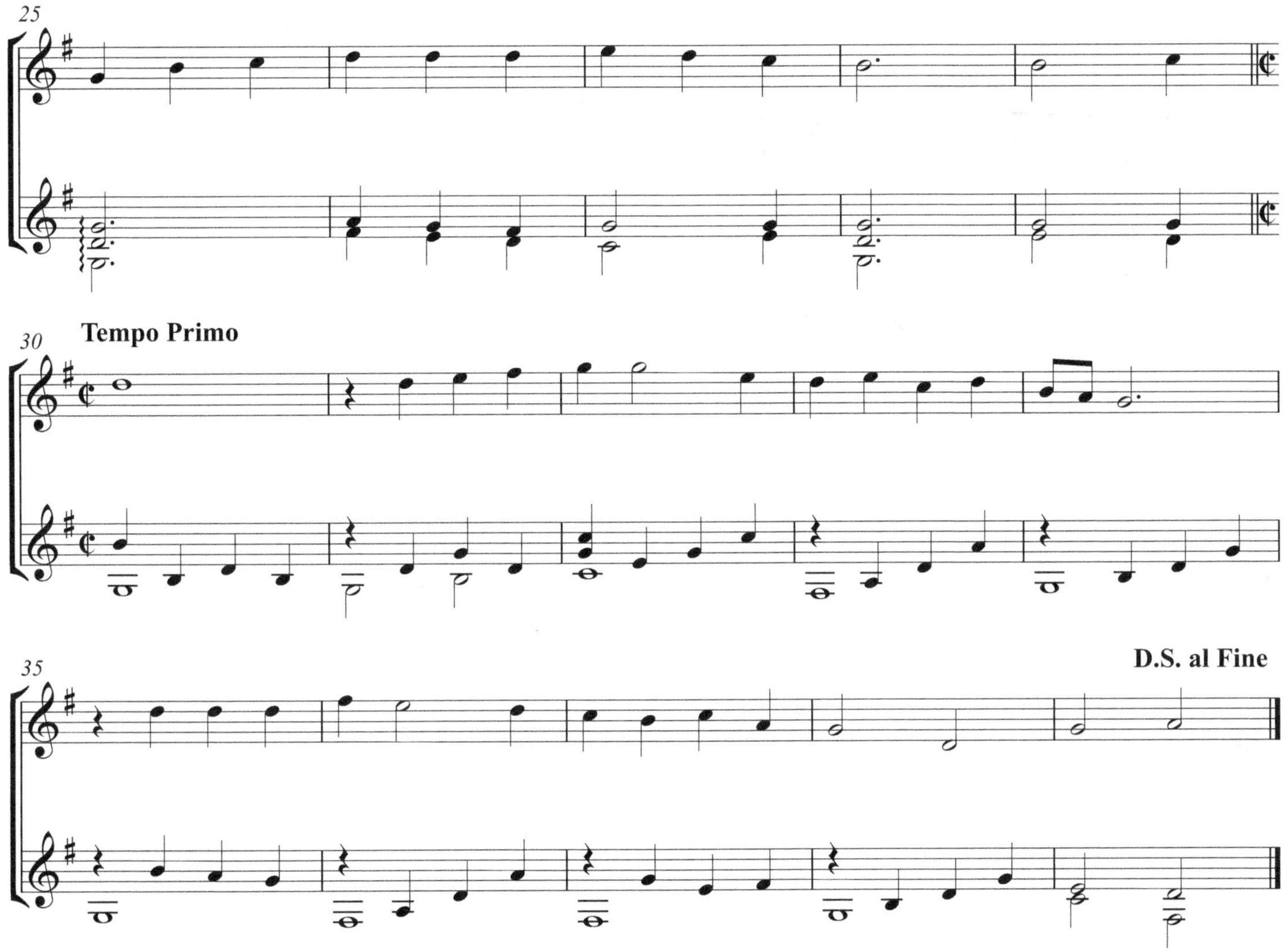

2

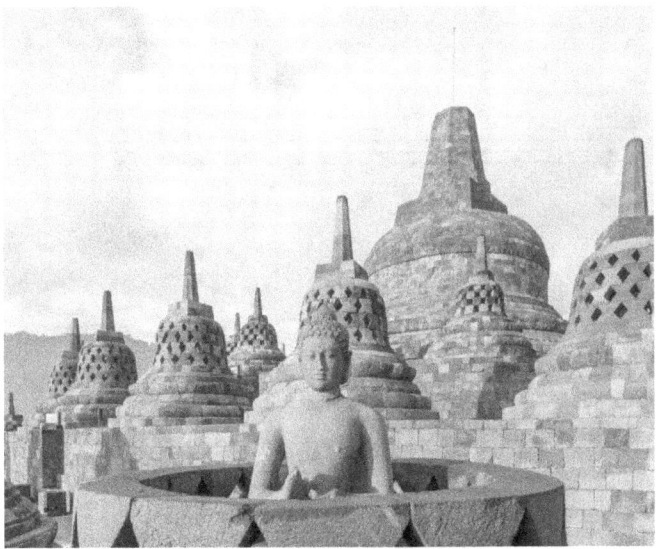

The Stupas of Borobudor, Java, Indonesia

The Colorado Trail

Traditional American

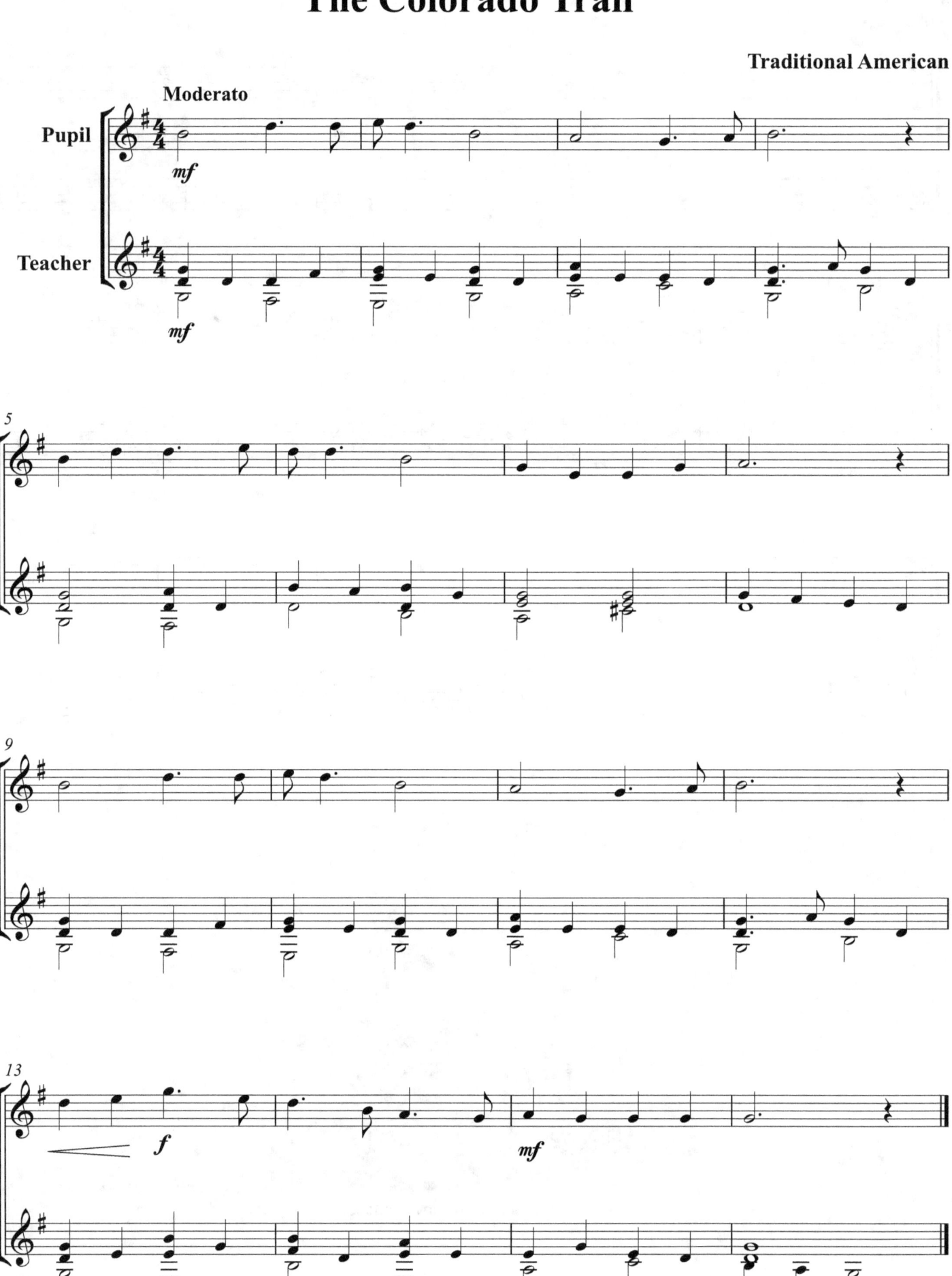

The Four Marys

Traditional Scottish

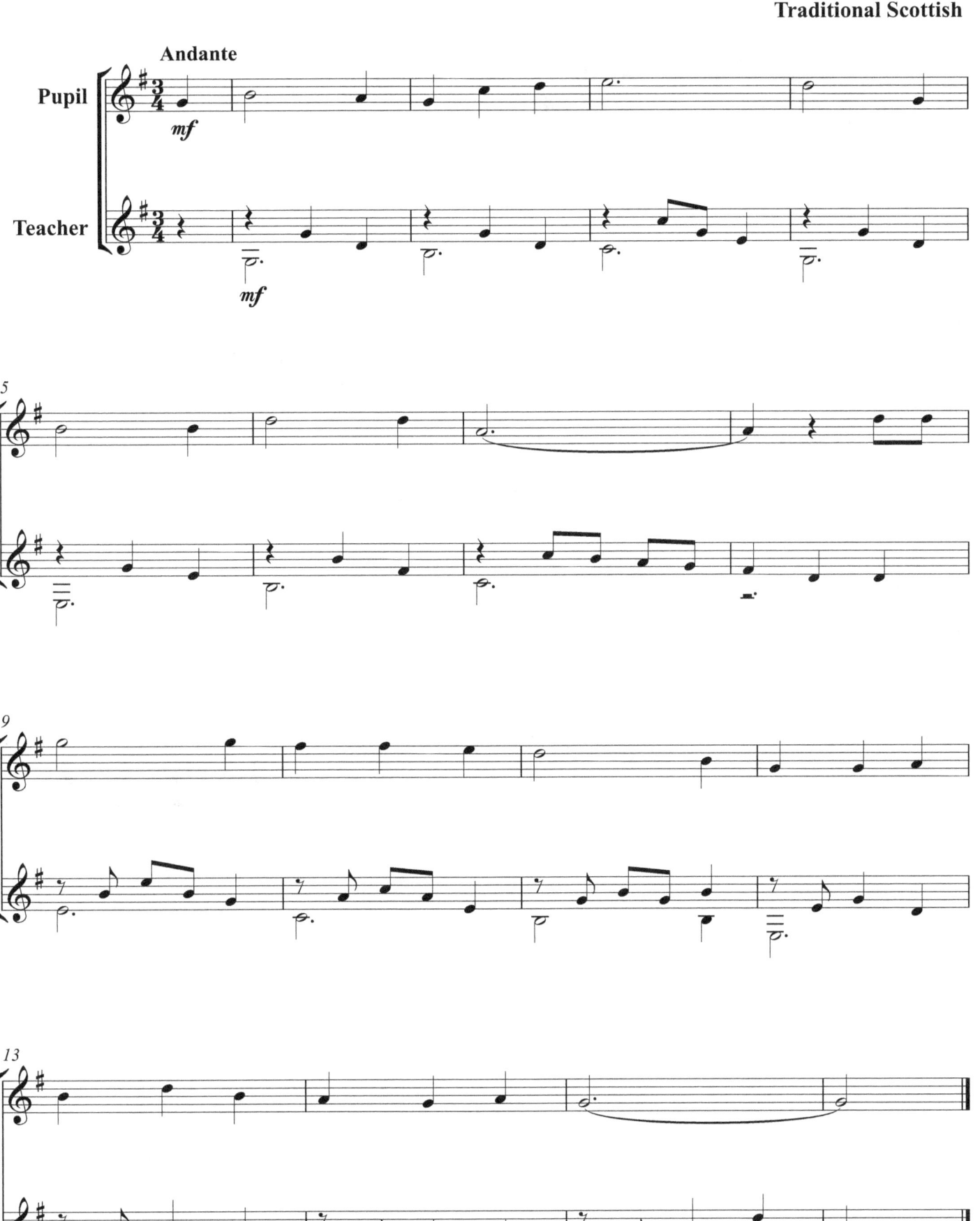

20

The Maid of Leko

Traditional German

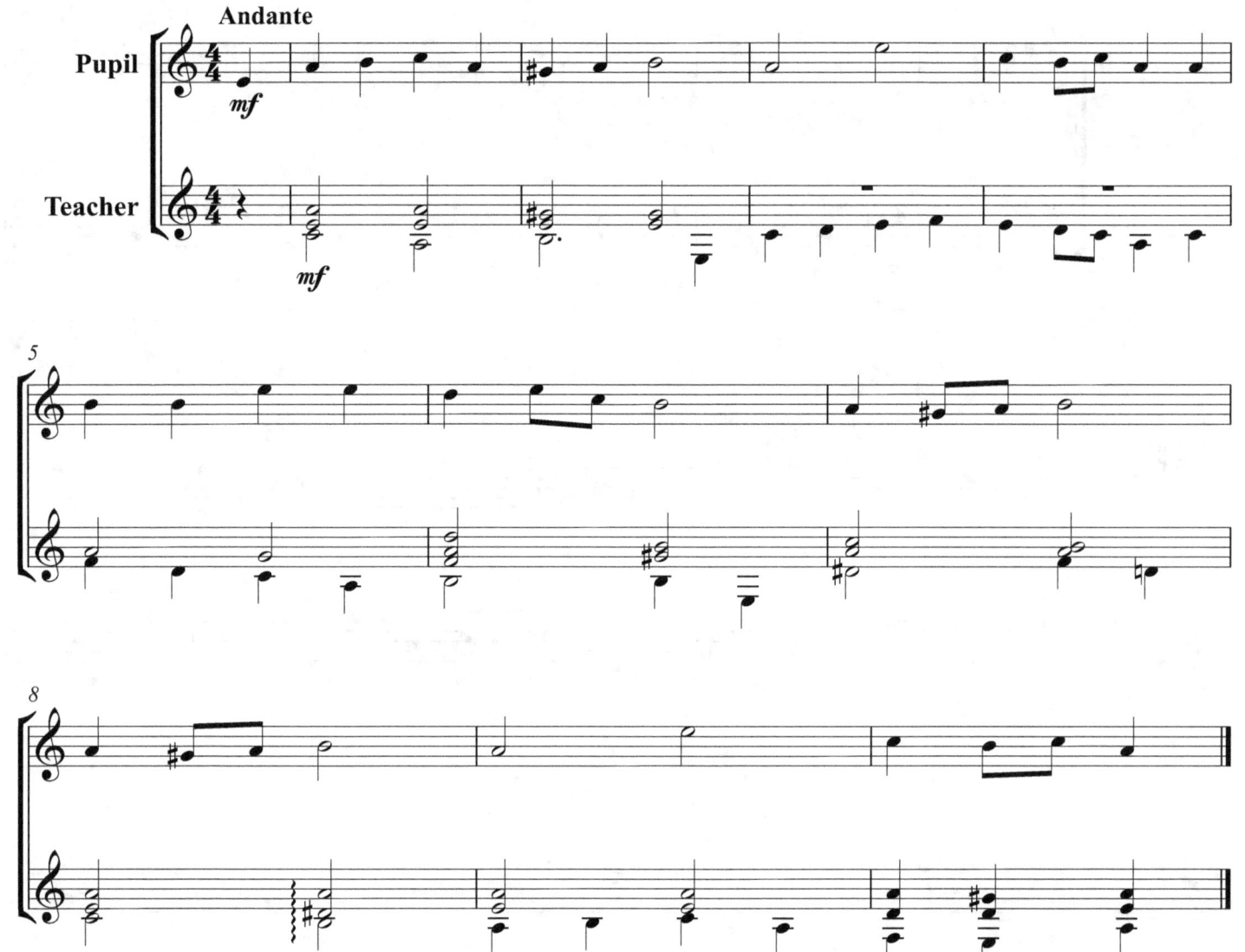

The Old Soldier

Traditional Greek

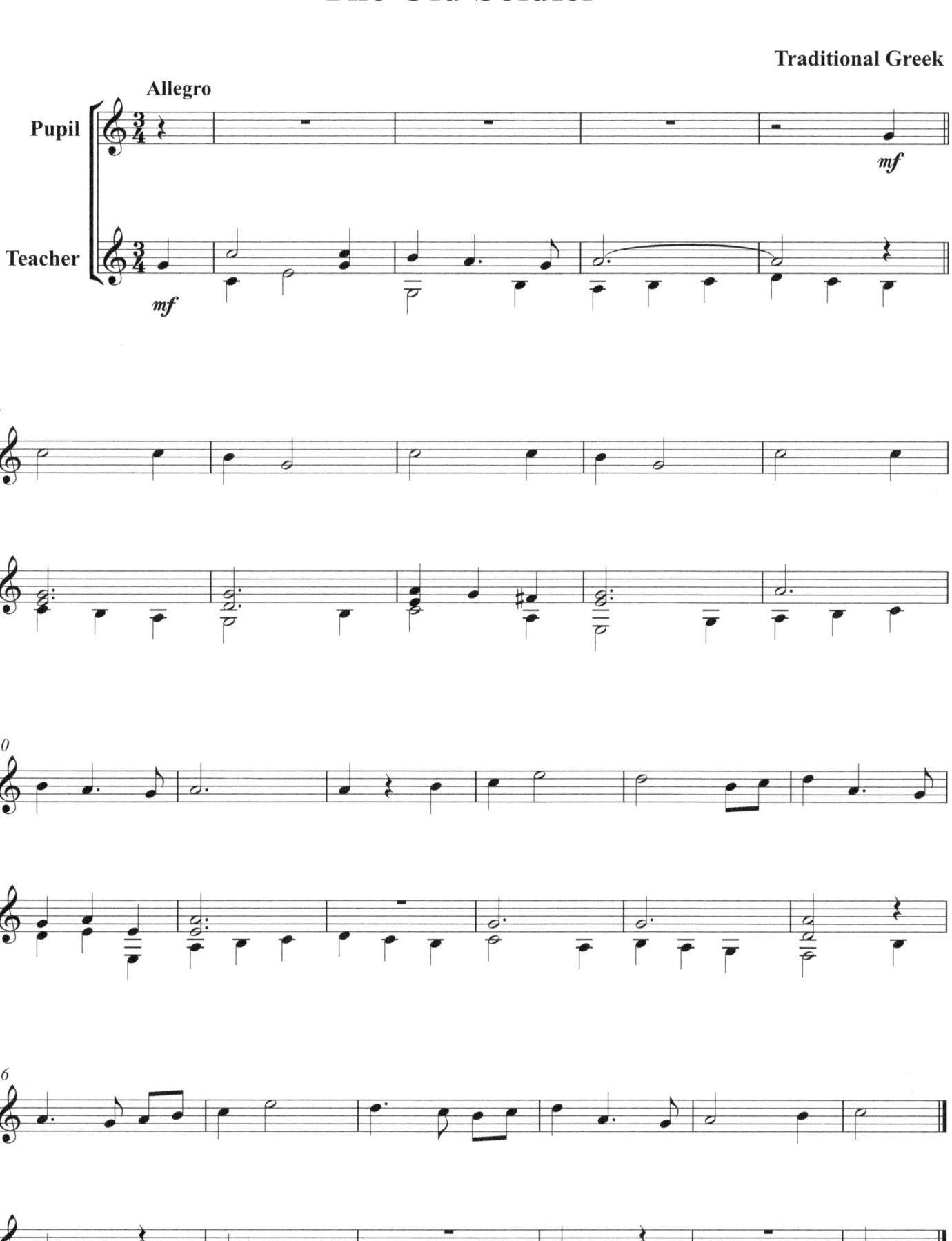

22

The Mountains Of Mourne

Traditional Irish

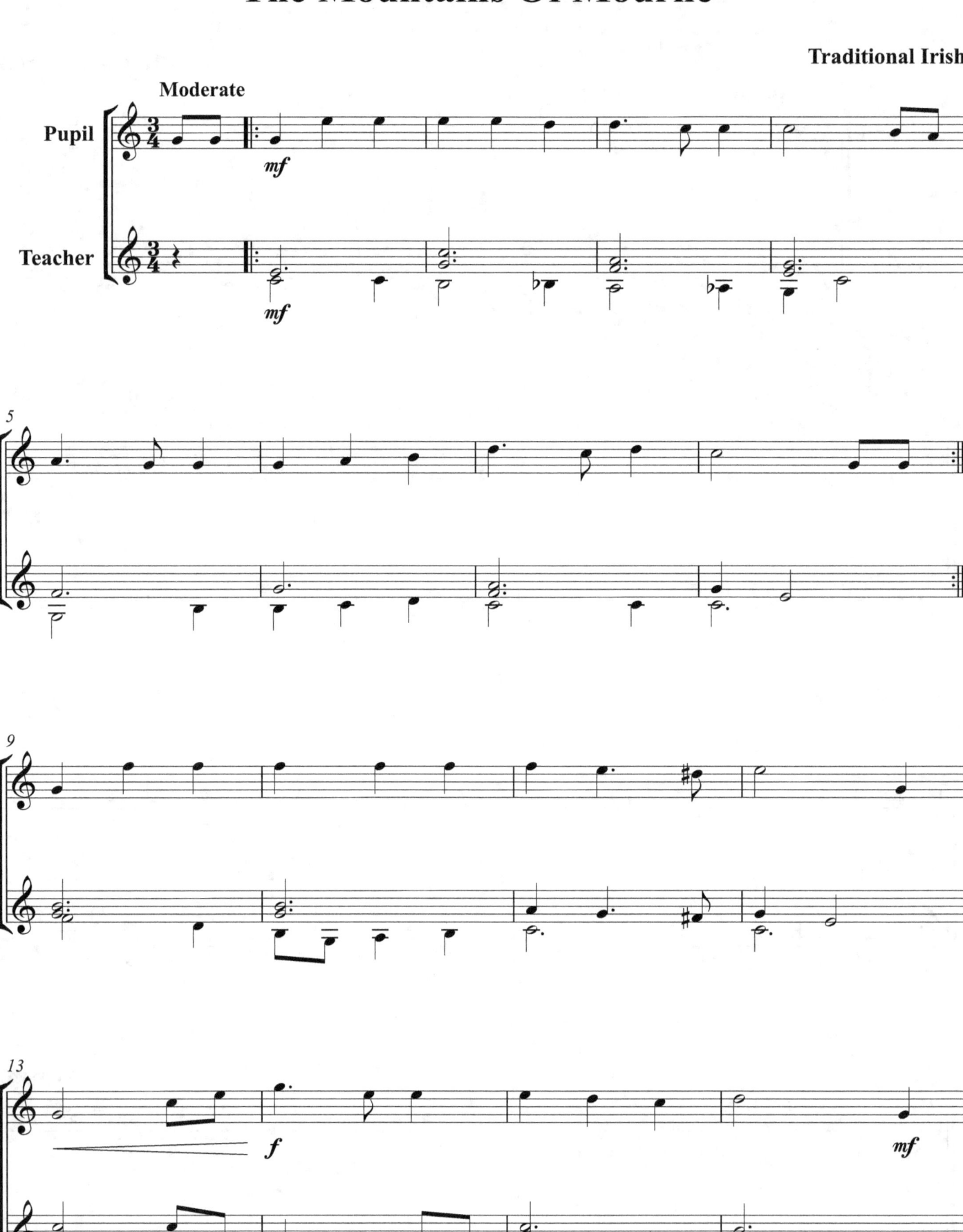

23

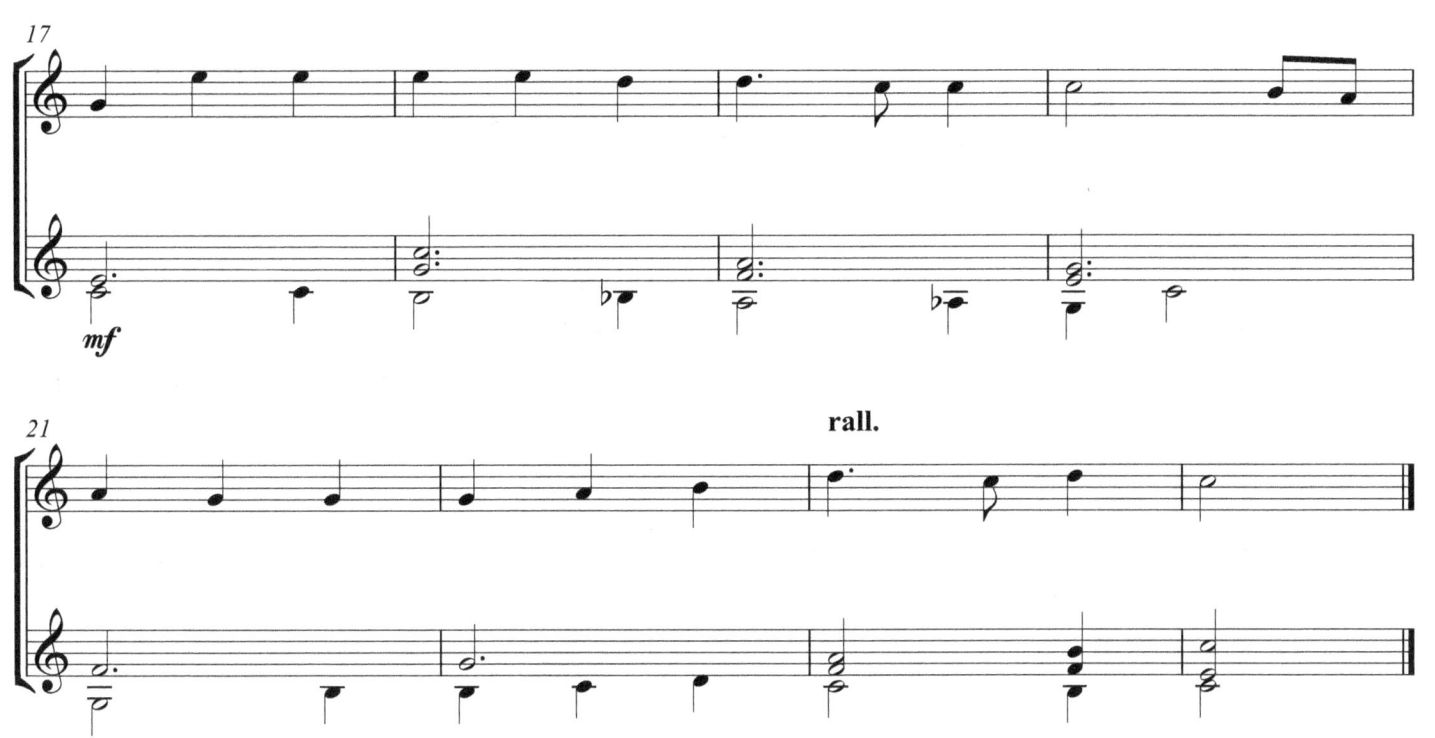

rall.

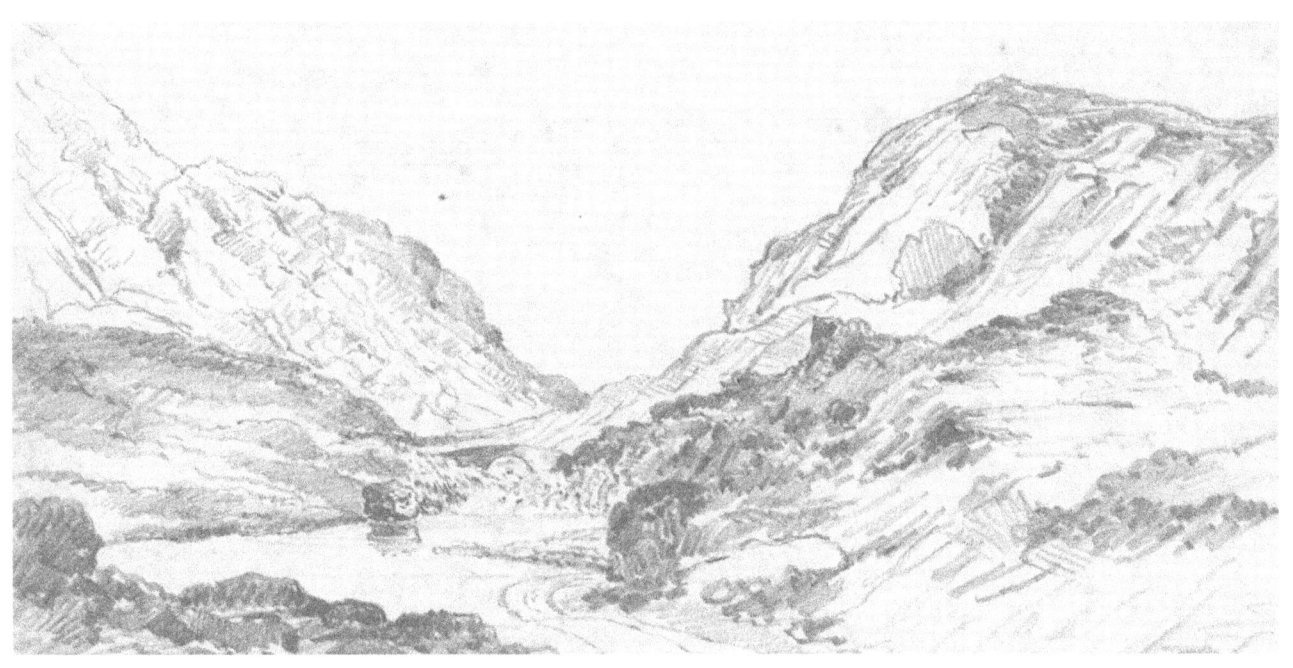

The Seeds Of Love

Traditional English

The Trees They Do Grow High

Traditional English

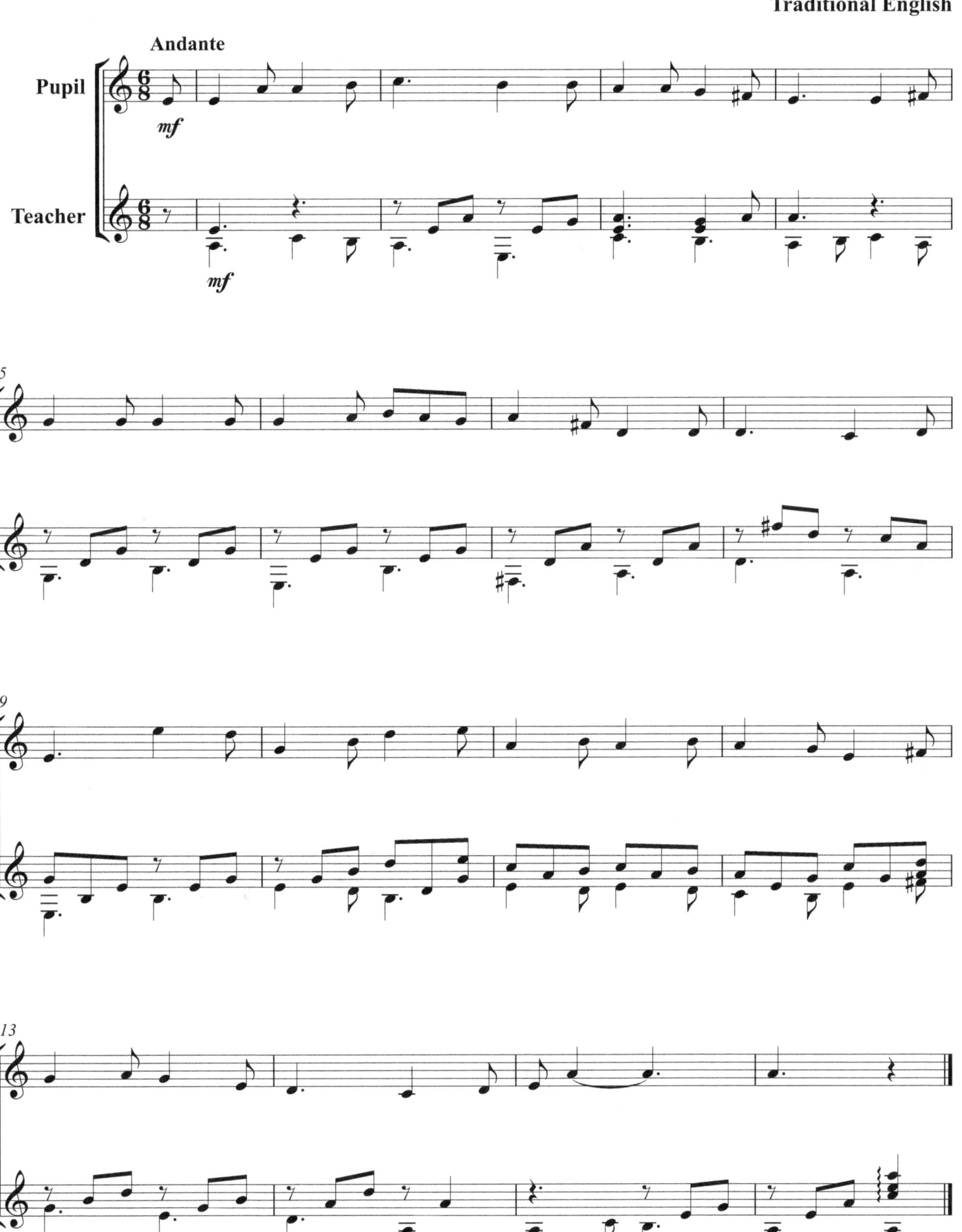

When Johnny Comes Marching Home

American Civil War Song

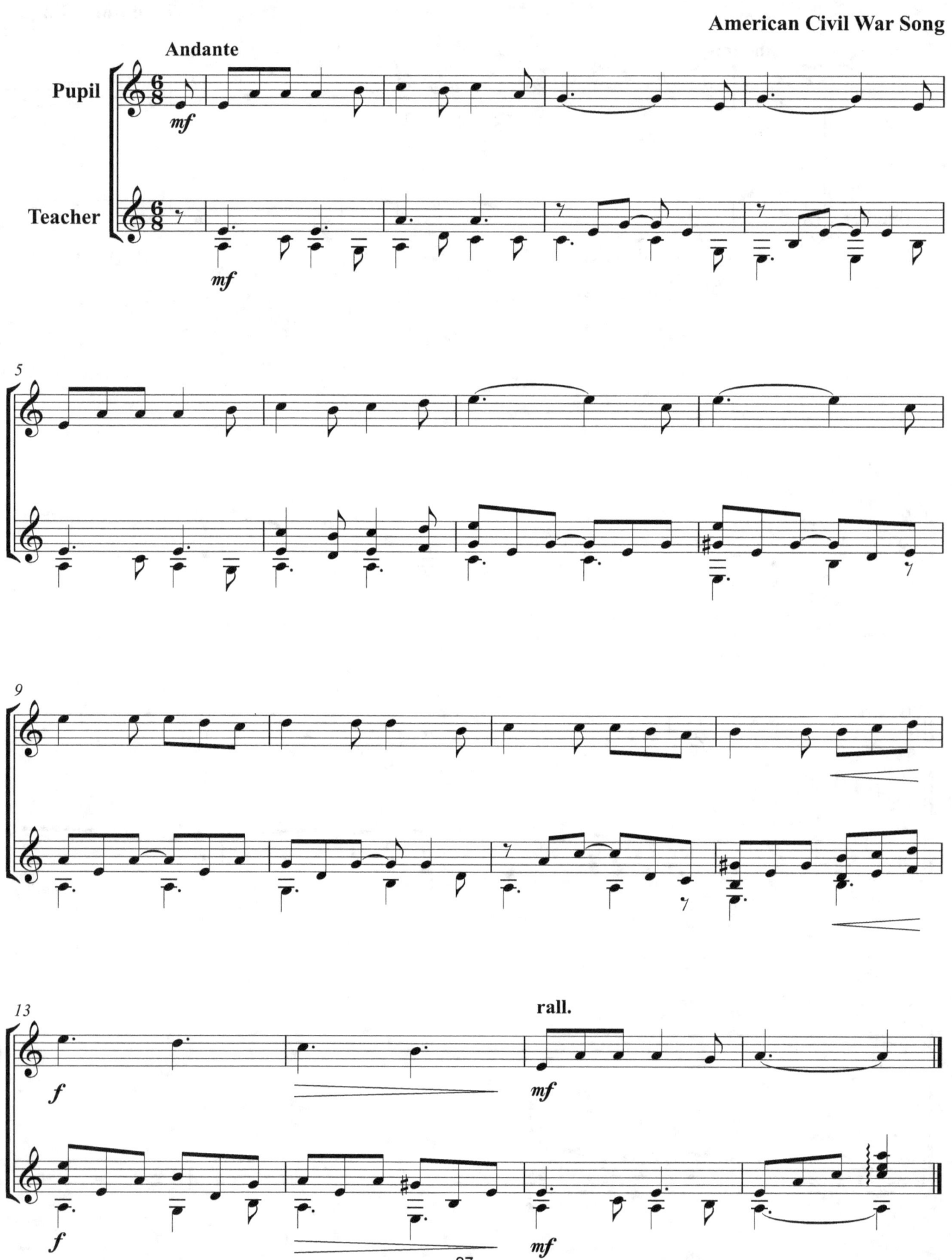

Whistle, Daughter, Whistle

Traditional American

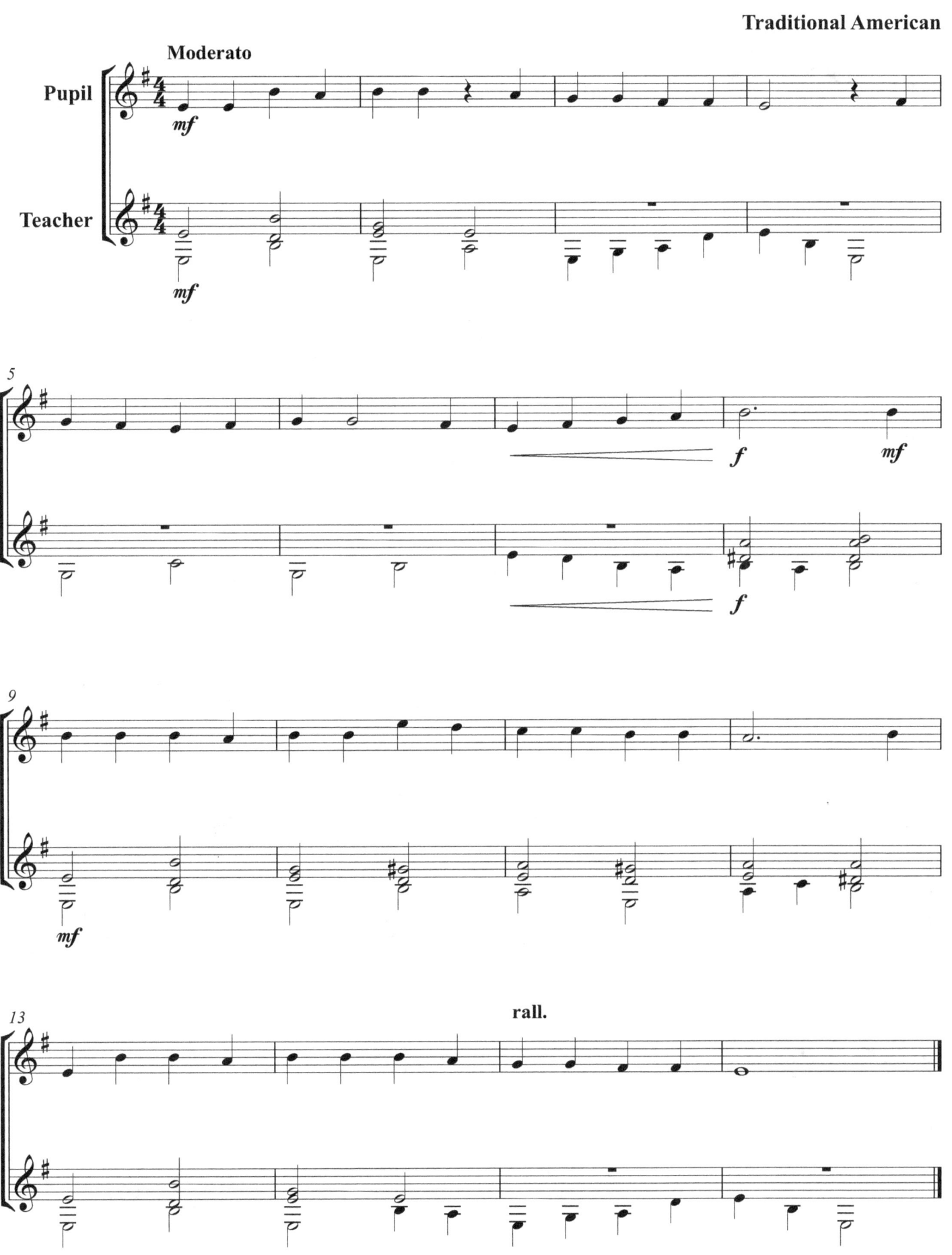

28

Wondrous Love

Traditional American

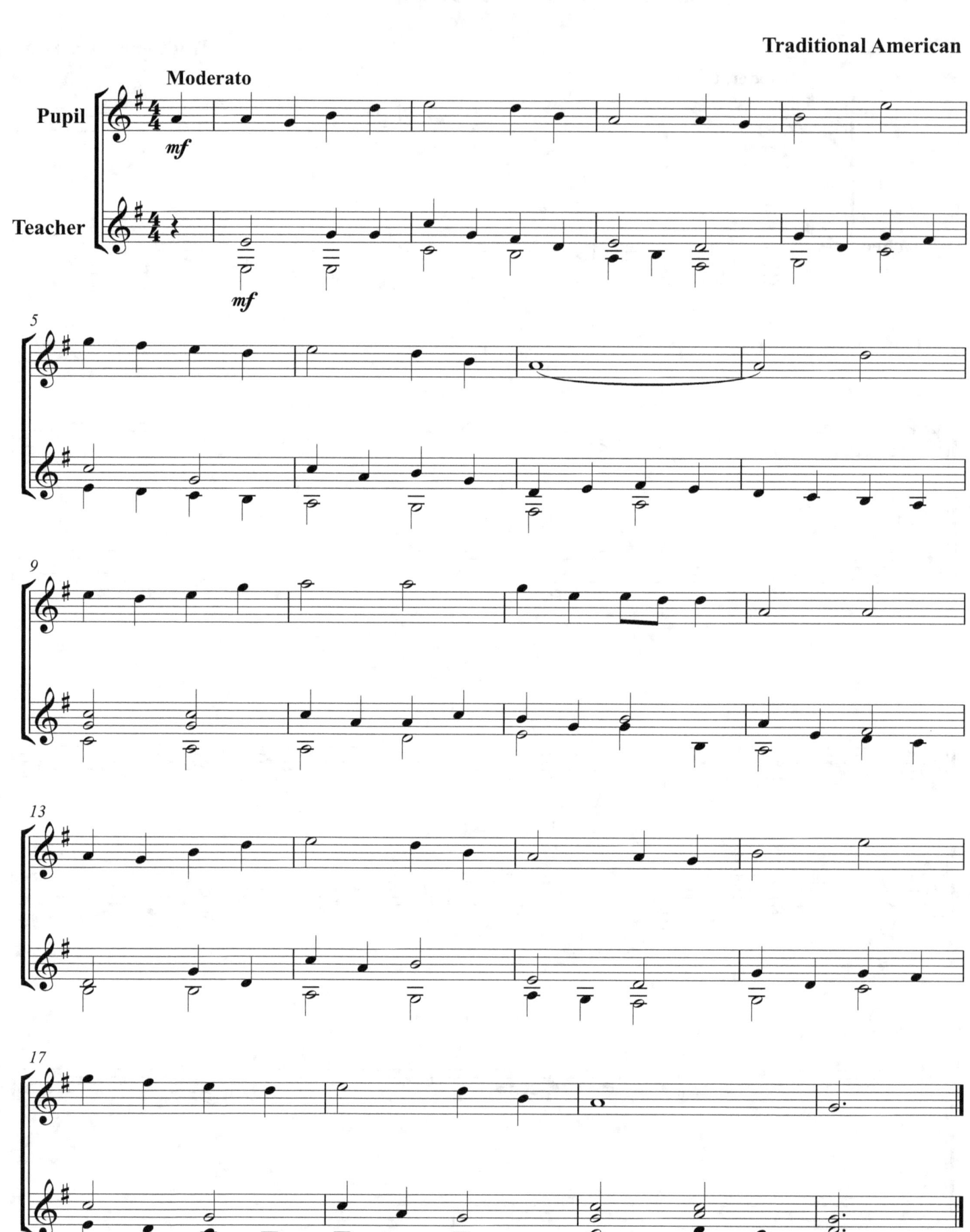

Also Available:

Meadow Music Publishing

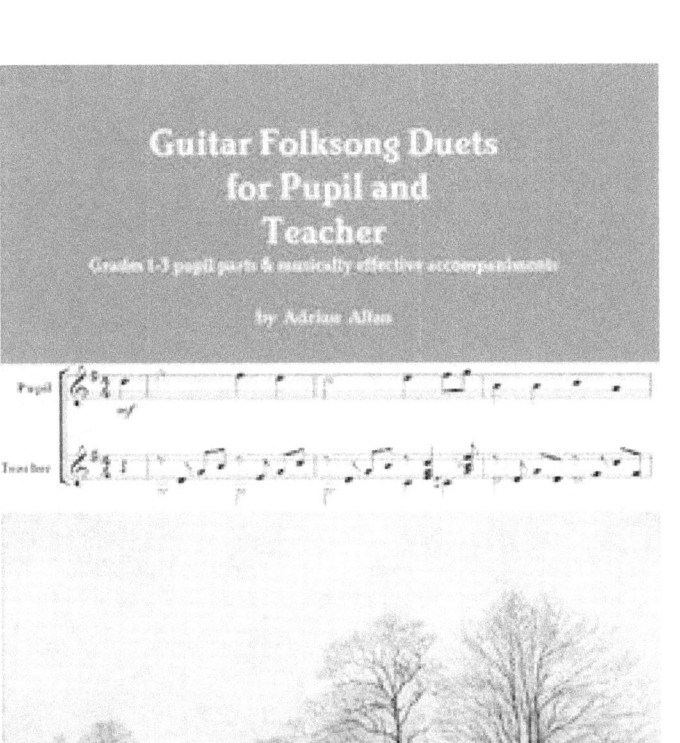

A collection of 19 folksong duets for teacher and pupil. The pupil parts are early grade and in the first positions. The teacher parts are musically effective and interesting to play.

Includes: Danny Boy, Down by the Sally Gardens, Ye Banks and Braes, The Lincolnshire Poacher, Bonny Mary of Argyle, Cockles and Mussels, An Eriskay Love Lilt, The Bluebells of Scotland, Men of Harlech, My Love is like a Red, Red Rose, On the Banks of Cairnie Burn, The Oak and the Ash, Allan Water, The Boar's Head Carol, Land of My Fathers, Drink to Me Only, The Leaving of Liverpool, Henry Martin, Annie Laurie.

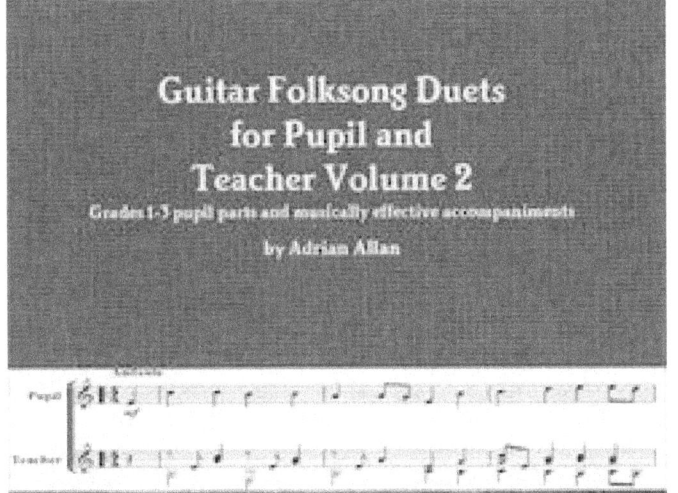

A second selection of guitar duets for pupil and teacher.

Included in this volume:

A Basque Lullaby; Beyond the Mountains; Early One Morning; Fishermen's Evening Song; Geordie; Golden Fish Swimming In the Lake; Goodnight; I Know Where I'm Going; I'm Seventeen Come Sunday; I Would Soothe You; Poor Old Horse; Robin Redbreast; Megan's Fair Daughter; O Vermeland; Santa Lucia; Shoes of Shining Leather; Shule Aroon; The Old Home; There Came a Little Stranger; The Lorelei; The Life That's Free; The Minstrel Boy; Will Ye Go, Lassie; Will Ye No' Come Back Again; Where the Gentian Blows

www.ingramcontent.com/pod-product-compliance
Lightning Source LLC
Chambersburg PA
CBHW081313180526
45170CB00007B/2684